A Word From the Editor

It has been said (and sung) that "it's a small world after all." It is not. In fact, Disney's world is so vast and has dining places so plentiful (there are hundreds of them) that picking the right spot to satisfy your group's diverse tastes can be a daunting experience.

It doesn't have to be. We assure you that whatever your palate prefers—simple or sublime, fast food or fine dining—it's being served up somewhere at Walt Disney World. Of course, finding (and reserving) the meal of your dreams can be a challenge. That's where this book comes in. If you're in search of a light snack or a filling lunch, a character breakfast or a champagne brunch—you'll find it described within these pages. You'll also discover rousing dinner shows, theme park favorites, quiet gems off the beaten path, and much more.

Given the popularity of many WDW eateries, booking a table in advance is nearly as important as selecting a venue. Our "WDW reservations" explanation will help you do just that.

Don't forget, you also need to be thinking about what you want to do later in the evening. Please, take your time, and when you're ready to strategize after-dinner entertainment, just flip to our Pubs and Lounges chapter. It delivers the scoop on

Downtown Disney and the BoardWalk entertainment zones, as well as compelling spots in the parks and resorts.

Rest assured, a lot of time and calories have gone into the creation of the dining guide you're holding. This is not merely an alphabetical restaurant listing—there are telephone books for that. Our hardy band of editorial gourmands has visited each and every establishment and sampled the fare. If we love a place, you'll know. If we agree that an eatery isn't worth a rave, it won't get one. But our opinions are just that, opinions. The truth is, one reader may see a giant turkey leg as a meal fit for a king, while the same snack leaves another feeling decidedly less regal. We understand that. Our goal is to provide all readers with the information necessary to ensure a successful Disney dining experience.

Chapters in this book are organized by Walt Disney World's parks and resort hotels, with one section focused on eateries within the Downtown Disney entertainment district, another devoted to dinner shows, and one focused on pubs and lounges. We've also included two bonus chapters: the first describes the Disney Dining Plan, and the second reveals some of the most revered and requested recipes in WDW history.

Dining establishments are noted for location, food quality and variety, and ambience. Within each entry there is a price rating and a listing of the meals served. Signature dishes may be listed, but menus (and chefs) do change, so if the braised lamb shank is *the* reason you're headed for a certain restaurant, it's best to call ahead.

If a seven-course gourmet meal is a crucial part of your vacation happiness, you're in luck. If you'd rather enjoy breakfast with Mickey Mouse or have lunch in a castle, you won't be disappointed. It's also possible to dine on couscous in Morocco,

BIRNBAUM GUIDES

2010

Walt Disney World DINING GUIDE

Wendy Lefkon
EDITORIAL DIRECTOR

Jill Safro
EDITOR

THE OFFICIAL GUIDE

Debbie Lofaso
DESIGNER

Jessica Ward
ASSISTANT EDITOR

Lois Spritzer and Pam Brandon
CONTRIBUTING WRITERS

Alexandra Mayes Birnbaum
CONSULTING EDITOR

A COMPLETE INSIDER'S GUIDE TO DINING DISNEY STYLE

DISNEY EDITIONS

NEW YORK

For Steve Birnbaum, who merely made all of this possible.

ISBN 978-1-4231-1703-2

Printed in the United States of America

Other 2010 Birnbaum's Official Disney Guides:

Disney Cruise Line
Disneyland
Walt Disney World
Walt Disney World For Kids
Walt Disney World Pocket Parks Guide
Walt Disney World Without Kids

FSC

Mixed Sources
Product group from well-managed forests, controlled sources and recycled wood or fibre

Cert no. SW-COC-002550
www.fsc.org
© 1996 Forest Stewardship Council

stroll to Germany for a knockwurst, to France for quiche, or to the United Kingdom for bangers and mash (don't turn up your nose—it's delicious). In other words, the gastronomic opportunities at Walt Disney World are bountiful, with nearly 6,000 different dishes on its collective menu. From appetizer to dessert, and even a nightcap, we hope this fills the bill.

Bon appétit!

HELPING HANDS

This book was made possible thanks to a tireless team of dedicated diners and behind-the-scenes support. Heartfelt thanks go to Judi Rosean, Peggy Arthur, Ned Waters, and Frankie LoBono. Special thanks to Karen Haynes and Pam Brandon, who have done so much to ensure the accuracy of Birnbaum's Official Walt Disney World Dining Guide.

Kudos to Erika Nein, copy editor extraordinaire. Thanks also to Jennifer Eastwood, Nisha Panchal, Michelle Olveira, and Claire Gunning for their editorial support and production panache.

Hats off to our volunteer tasters: Margaret Verdon, Linda Verdon, Trace Schielzo, Irene Safro, Roy Safro, Mike Carroll, Joan Peterson, Brendan Carroll, and Heather Pommerencke.

Acknowledgments would be incomplete without mentioning our founding editor, Steve Birnbaum, who continues to be an inspiration for us all, as well as Alexandra Mayes Birnbaum, who is both a guiding light and careful reader of every word.

Table of Contents

A GUIDE TO THIS GUIDE

This book is a comprehensive guide, with details about each and every eatery on Walt Disney World property. Rather than present you with a book of epic proportions, we've labored to keep the project pocket-sized by combining concise descriptions with handy symbols. Each restaurant entry is preceded by a symbol that indicates whether the establishment is a fast-food spot or a table-service restaurant. We've also indicated whether or not said restaurant is a participant in the Disney Dining Plan (see page 13 for details). Here's a rundown of the symbols:

- 🏃 = Fast Food (aka quick service)
- 🍽 = Table Service
- 🔴 = Disney Dining Plan participant
- **B** = Breakfast
- **L** = Lunch
- **D** = Dinner
- **S** = Snack
- **$** = Under $15
- **$$** = $15–$36
- **$$$** = $36–$60
- **$$$$** = $60 and up

Prices are *estimates* based on an average adult dinner consisting of a soft drink, entrée, and either one appetizer, side order, or dessert *before* tax and tip. (Breakfast and lunch generally cost less.)

How to Book a WDW Table

The guide you are holding will help you select an ideal locale in which to enjoy every Walt Disney World meal. Picking the perfect place, however, is merely step one in the Disney dining experience. We cannot overemphasize the importance of the follow-up step: *booking* it—well in advance. For an explanation of WDW's unique reservations system, turn the page.

Walt Disney World Reservations

Walt Disney World has reservations about reservations. It seems the traditional system inevitably led to delays, thanks to no-shows and late-comers. As a means of expediting matters, Disney modified the process. Essentially, this means that you arrange to receive priority treatment when it comes to being seated at an agreed upon time. Here's how it works: Call to request a time at a table-service eatery; arrive about 10 to 15 minutes before the assigned time and check in; receive the next available table that can accommodate your party. (There may be a wait involved.)

If an eatery accepts reservations, make them. Times can be secured up to 180 days ahead by calling 407-WDW-DINE (939-3463). Hours are 7 A.M. to 10 P.M. If you are unable to book ahead of time, try to make same-day arrangements. Many restaurants will accommodate walk-ins who are willing to wait (just don't arrive starving!).

Disney resorts often have a phone in the lobby area that provides direct contact with the "Dine Line." Simply touch 55—the call is toll-free. From theme park pay phones, touch *88 (also toll-free). Otherwise, call 407-WDW-DINE.

Hot Tip

At press time, dining prices for "kids" covered guests ages 3 through 9. Most WDW table-service eateries have special menus just for little ones. Fast-food establishments offer special kid-friendly items, too.

For same-day arrangements in the Magic Kingdom, go to City Hall; in Epcot, head to Guest Relations; in Disney's Hollywood Studios, go to the corner of Hollywood and Sunset; in Animal Kingdom, ask at Guest Relations. Bookings can be made at Downtown Disney Guest Relations. Of course, plans can also be made at the restaurants themselves.

Keep in mind that a WDW restaurant reservation is not a traditional reservation. You may have to wait a while when you arrive at your assigned time. Rest assured, your party will be given the first table that opens up.

WHAT DO YOU THINK?

No contribution is of greater value to us in preparing the next edition of this book than your comments on what we have written and on your own Walt Disney World dining experiences. Please share your thoughts and insights with us by writing to:

Jill Safro, Editor
Birnbaum's Walt Disney World Dining Guide 2010
Disney Editions
114 Fifth Avenue, 14th Floor
New York, NY 10011

Note that WDW dinner shows (page 113) must be booked in advance. The Hoop-Dee-Doo Musical Revue, the Spirit of Aloha dinner show, and Mickey's Backyard Barbecue accept requests up to 180 days in advance.

Finally, the Disney dining scene is ever-evolving and procedures tend to change, so we advise calling 407-WDW-DINE to confirm current reservation policies.

NO RESERVATIONS? GOOD LUCK!

Disney's reservations system may allow for walk-ins (who are willing to wait). That said, the popularity of the Disney Dining Plan has made spontaneity something of a challenge. If you get caught without reservations during peak dining hours, consider eating a little earlier or later than the masses usually do. Call 407-WDW-DINE and ask about seating availability. In the meantime, here are a few of our favorite table-service places to pop into without an advance reservation (though there is usually a wait involved):

• Biergarten (Epcot)
• Big River Grille & Brewing Works (BoardWalk)
• ESPN Club (BoardWalk)
• Hollywood Brown Derby (Disney's Hollywood Studios)
• House of Blues (Downtown Disney, West Side; 407-934-BLUE)
• Il Mulino New York Trattoria (Swan)
• Portobello (Downtown Disney, Pleasure Island)
• Raglan Road (Downtown Disney, Pleasure Island)
• Yachtsman Steakhouse (Yacht Club)

Disney Dining Plan

To some, it may sound too good to be true: enjoy the convenience of pre-paid meals and stretch your vacation dollar by up to about 30 percent in the process. But the Disney Dining Plan is just that—a package "add-on" that lets guests redeem meal credits at more than 100 on-property eateries and, by doing so, actually save a few bucks. The plan is flexible, too. Feeling famished? Have an extra snack or a whole meal today and skip one tomorrow. Want to be waited on hand and foot all day? Throw caution to the wind and cash in three table-service meals. Of course, that means you'll have an abundance of quick-service experiences in your future, but who cares? You're on vacation. Do what makes you happy. To learn more about the Disney Dining Plan, turn the page.

The Dining Plan is available to any guest staying at any resort that's owned and operated by Walt Disney World. (That means all resorts on WDW property, with the exception of the Swan, Dolphin, Buena Vista Palace, Best Western Lake Buena Vista, Doubletree Guest Suites, Regal Sun, Hilton, Holiday Inn, and Hotel Royal Plaza.) The plan, which starts at about $40 a day for adults, *must be purchased at the same time the resort is booked*. Together, the room and the dining plan are known as the Magic Your Way Plus Dining package. Here's what's included in the basic Dining Plan (there are also Deluxe, Quick Service, Premium, and Platinum packages):

- One "Table Service" meal (includes buffets) per person, per night of the package stay.
- One "Quick Service" meal per person, per night of the package.
- One snack per person, per night of stay.

In other words, if you are booked for 6 nights at, say, the Polynesian or any other Disney owned-and-operated resort, you are entitled to 6 table-service meals, 6 quick-service meals, and 6 snacks during your stay.

One Table Service Meal includes an entrée, dessert (except at breakfast) and a non-alcoholic beverage, *or* one full buffet plus soft drink. One non-alcoholic specialty beverage may be substituted for dessert.

Hot Tip

Just because your meals are pre-paid, it doesn't mean they're pre-booked! Make reservations for table-service restaurants by calling 407-WDW-DINE (939-3463).

Hot Tip

One Quick Service Meal includes an entrée, dessert (dessert is for lunch and dinner only), and a non-alcoholic beverage, or one complete combo meal, plus one dessert (lunch and dinner), and a single serving of a soft drink.

One Snack consists of any of the following:
• Frozen ice-cream novelty, ice pop, or fruit bar
• Popcorn scoop (single-serving box)
• Single piece of whole fruit
• Single-serving bag of snacks
• 20-ounce bottle of soda or water
• Medium fountain soft drink
• 12-ounce coffee, tea, or hot chocolate
• Single serving of pre-packaged milk or juice

When it comes time for a meal or a snack, be sure to present your hotel room key (aka your "key to the world" card) before ordering. That way your server will know to charge meals to your Disney Dining Plan. Tax is included, but gratuity is not. Please remember to tip your server!

Each time you redeem meals or snacks from the plan, your server or cashier will give you a receipt showing the remaining balance on your Dining Plan. For example, if your party of four started with 20 table-service meals and everyone in the group used one table-service meal, your receipt would indicate a balance of 16 table-service meals for the remainder of your stay.

DISNEY DINING PLAN

Hot Tip

A "quick-service only" Dining Plan is a cost-efficient option. It starts at about $20 per person, per day and includes 2 quick-service meals and 2 snacks a day. Everyone on the plan gets a refillable mug.

Snack credits must be redeemed at participating Walt Disney World locations. In this book, we've indicated these establishments by placing a 💖 by each restaurant. However, as specifics may change, we recommend visiting *www.disneyworld.com* or calling 407-939-3463 for updates.

Finally, be aware that unused meals expire at midnight on your package reservation check-out date. So, on the last day of your trip, eat like there's no tomorrow! Note that table-service items are meant to be consumed on-site. In other words, please don't request a giant doggie bag.

SIGNATURE RESTAURANTS

The following "Signature" restaurants, dinner shows, and character dining experiences require guests to redeem *two credits* when using the Disney Dining Plan: Jiko—The Cooking Place, Flying Fish Cafe, California Grill, Hollywood Brown Derby, Hoop-Dee-Doo Musical Revue, Mickey's Backyard Barbecue, Cítricos, Narcoossee's, The Spirit of Aloha, Artist Point, Yachtsman Steakhouse, Cinderella's Royal Table, and private dining (room service).

Magic Kingdom

A lot has changed since Walt Disney World's original theme park opened in 1971. Back then, when it came to quelling hunger pangs, it was pretty much burger or bust. Nowadays, the options are a lot more diverse—with everything from egg rolls to cinnamon rolls, smoked turkey legs to chicken Marsala, clam chowder to coconut fried shrimp. Regardless of your tastes or budget, the seven "lands" in the Magic Kingdom boast a bounty of palate pleasers for the whole family.

17

ADVENTURELAND

🏃 Aloha Isle

`S` `$`

Switzerland meets Hawaii (hey, this *is* the
Magic Kingdom) at this snack stand across
from the Swiss Family Treehouse. Stop here
for all things pineapple—juice, spears, floats,
and the perennial favorite, the Dole Whip
frozen pineapple soft-serve dessert. This spot
has been around forever—they're definitely
doing something right.

🏃 El Pirata y el Perico

`L S` `$-$$` 🔾

Though its name translates as "The Pirate
and the Parrot," you won't find pirates or
parrots at this shady stop across from Pirates
of the Caribbean. Instead, you can munch on
beef and vegetarian tacos and taco salads.
The venue operates seasonally, so it may not
be open during your visit.

🏃 Sunshine Tree Terrace

`S` `$`

After you visit the Enchanted Tiki Room—
Under New Management or fly on a magic
carpet, you can take a cool break with some
of the chilliest snacks in the park—citrus
swirls (soft serve swirled with orange slush)
and slushes (orange- or lemon-flavored).
Cappuccino, iced cappuccino, cappuccino
floats, espresso, and soft drinks round out
the menu. A Walt Disney World staple, the
Sunshine Tree has been dishing out treats to
Magic Kingdom guests for as long as we
can remember.

FANTASYLAND

🍴 Cinderella's Royal Table
B L D **$$$** ❤

You don't have to be a prince or a princess to eat like one. At least, not here in the Magic Kingdom. This regal establishment, tucked inside Cinderella Castle, is a high-ceilinged re-creation of a majestic mead hall. It's small as Disney restaurants go, but there's no feeling cramped—thanks to a limited number of tables and towering windows that overlook Fantasyland. It's definitely the most upscale eatery in this kingdom, but for many, it's worth every royal penny.

Cinderella welcomes guests into her home for three meals a day and greets them in the castle lobby, while her princess friends mingle in the dining room at breakfast and lunch (Fairy Godmother spreads her magic at all meals). Dinner guests can feast on dishes such as prime rib or pan-seared salmon, plus mashed potatoes and a fresh veggie side. Breakfast and lunch fare tends to be upstaged by Cinderella and friends. The *enormously* popular all-you-can-eat meals tend to book up the full 180 days ahead, leaving no room for spontaneity. (See page 21 for details on booking.)

The Once Upon a Time Breakfast costs about $35 for adults, $24 for kids ages 3 through 9. The price includes the Princess Photo Package (see page 22). The Fairytale Lunch costs about $38 for adults, $25 for kids ages 3 through 9, including the Princess Photo Package. The evening meal is called the Dreams Come True Dinner. In addition to a tableside visit by Fairy Godmother, it includes an appetizer, entrée, beverage, and

Hot Tip

The Magic Kingdom is a dry kingdom. Guests in search of drinks of a more spirited variety need look no further than beyond the Magic Kingdom's borders. Cocktails are served everywhere else at WDW.

dessert. Dinner costs about $43 for adults, $27 for kids and includes the photo package. Reservations are a must. Call exactly *180 days in advance*, first thing in the morning (7 A.M. Eastern Standard Time), and keep your fingers crossed. (Guests staying at a Disney World resort should read the Hot Tip on page 11.)

Enchanted Grove

S $

What's enchanted about this snack shack is its ability to cool you off with a lemonade, lemon slush, or a strawberry-vanilla ice cream soft-serve swirl. It's on a path that borders Tomorrowland and is easy to miss—so pay attention!

Mrs. Potts' Cupboard

S $

Ice cream fans will appreciate this walk-up window near the Many Adventures of Winnie the Pooh. It offers soft-serve cones, hot fudge, strawberry shortcake, and brownie sundaes, plus shakes and floats.

Pinocchio Village Haus

L D S $-$$

One of the better spots to target with kids in tow is Pinocchio Village Haus. It's a Small World's next-door neighbor seems small from the outside, but don't be fooled by

TOUGHEST TICKETS IN TOWN

Cinderella's Royal Table character dining is—hands down—the most difficult reservation to secure at Disney World. Why? For starters, Cinderella is one popular princess. And there's the allure of dining in the castle—the most famous landmark in the world's most popular theme park. Add to that the fact that the restaurant is small (122 seats), and you end up with a supply-and-demand issue.

The good news is, thanks to a change in policy and the addition of a princess-hosted lunch, it's gotten slightly less impossible to snag a seat at Cinderella's table. Potential guests still reserve by calling 407-WDW-DINE (939-3463) 180 days ahead, but now they must pay for the meal at the same time the reservation is booked. There is no charge for infants, but they must be included in the reservation.

Expect your credit card to be charged immediately upon making the reservation. Cancellations or changes must be made at least 24 hours prior to the reservation to receive a refund. The only one who can change or cancel a reservation is the one whose name is on the card.

Reservations cannot be transferred, and the lead name may not change.

Guests must present the credit card that was used to book the reservation, but may charge the meal to a different card or the Disney Dining Plan.

Continued on page 22

appearances: there's a half-dozen dining rooms inside. One room boasts picture windows that overlook the It's a Small World loading area. It's fun to watch the boats bob by as you munch on lunch. It's a good place to take kids (or picky eaters) for lunch, dinner, or snacks. They offer pizza, chicken nuggets, salads, fries, and soft drinks. This is a popular destination in a bustling neighborhood, so you may want to go a little before or after traditional mealtime rush hours.

Continued from page 21

If your vacation package includes meals, you'll still have to make a reservation with a credit card. Make sure you tell the fine folks at WDW-DINE all about your package, including the confirmation number.

Finally, a word about the Photo Package: A cast member will snap a photo of your party with Cinderella inside the castle lobby. By the end of your meal, you'll receive a package including four 4-by-6-inch prints and one 6-by-8-inch print of your group, plus one 6-by-8-inch print of the castle. The photo package is included with the price of the meal.

Whew! That's a lot of work for one dining experience. Is it worth it? Judging by the smiles we see day in and day out, we have to say yes. Breaking bread in Cinderella's home is, for many, a memory of a lifetime. (Just don't tell kids about the experience until you've secured a reservation!)

Hot Tip

The hours from 11 A.M. to 2 P.M., and again from about 5 P.M. to 7 P.M., are mealtime rush hours in the Magic Kingdom. Try to eat earlier or later whenever possible.

Scuttle's Landing

S **$**

This snack stand near Dumbo the Flying Elephant serves up frozen carbonated beverages and soft drinks. The frozen treat is simple, but refreshing—especially if the weather's warm and you find yourself thinking "nothing would hit the spot like some sweet, Technicolor ice." Kids love it.

The Village Fry Shoppe

L D S **$**

A trip to this walk-up window, located near Mrs. Potts' Cupboard, can yield hot dogs, fries, soft drinks, and snacks such as carrot cake and apple caramel dippers.

FRONTIERLAND

Pecos Bill Cafe

L D S **$-$$** ♥

Pecos Bill—a classic "oldie but goody"—has been feeding hungry cowpokes for more than three decades. The look has changed a bit over time, but the reliable quality of the vittles remains. Cheeseburgers, sandwiches, chili, salads, and french fries are the staples.

(If you'd rather skip the fries, ask for an à la carte version or an apple slice substitute.)

What sets this spot apart from other burger establishments? Two words: fixin's bar. It's full of items with which to garnish your meal. Among them: lettuce and tomato, and freshly sautéed mushrooms and onions.

The lines grow long during mealtimes. Resist the urge to jump on the first queue you hit and head toward a cashier that's farther from the entrance. The line may be shorter. This is one of the most popular fast-food restaurants in the Magic Kingdom—it's high on our list of favorites, too.

LIBERTY SQUARE

Columbia Harbour House

L D S $-$$

Few would expect such a lovely setting in which to snack on tuna and vegetarian sandwiches (on whole grain bread), chicken strips, chili, salad, fried fish, or New England clam chowder (no longer served in a bread bowl, but still popular), but Disney has done this fast-food emporium up in style—complete with antiques, model ships,

Hot Tip

To avoid lines, eat lunch or dinner at a Magic Kingdom restaurant that takes reservations—Tony's Town Square, Crystal Palace, Plaza Restaurant, Liberty Tree Tavern, or Cinderella's Royal Table. Know that you may have to wait a few minutes once you arrive at the eatery.

harpoons, nautical instruments, and even lace tieback curtains. Whether it's lunch or dinner, this is a charming stop. In addition to the chowder, we stand by the Lighthouse sandwich (hummus with tomato and broccoli slaw) and the Anchors Away tuna sandwich.

Liberty Tree Tavern
L D **$$$** ❤

Step back in time at this early American tavern where the decor has a tendency to outdazzle the fare. Here, the wallpaper looks as if it might have come from Colonial Williamsburg, the curtains hang from cloth loops, and the rooms are filled with mementos that might have been found in the homes of Thomas Jefferson, George Washington, and Ben Franklin. The restaurant is located across from the Hall of Presidents attraction.

The à la carte lunch menu includes fish, pot roast, turkey, clam chowder, sandwiches, and soups. Dinner is an all-you-can-eat affair—salad, roast turkey, flank steak, pork chops, mac and cheese, and more—served family-style. The cost for dinner is about $30 for adults, $15 for children ages 3 through 9. Dessert is included; specialty beverages are not. Despite the tavern motif, no alcohol is served (this kingdom is not only magic, it's dry). The restaurant is hosted by Stouffer's (expect a preponderance of their products). Reservations are recommended. *Disney characters were not in attendance at press time, but that may change. Call 407-WDW-DINE (939-3643) for updates.*

Sleepy Hollow
S **$**

Often missed by guests rushing toward the Haunted Mansion or other Magic Kingdom hot spots, this underappreciated dessert window has a lot to offer: ice-cream cookie sandwiches, fresh-baked cookies, funnel cakes, caramel corn, and more are the sweets for sale here. It's in the Hall of Presidents neighborhood near the Liberty Square bridge. Eat on the adjacent brick patio and get a view of Cinderella Castle at no extra charge.

MAIN STREET, U.S.A.

Casey's Corner

L D S $ ♥

Casey's is a grand slam for baseball fans—and those who just happen to love the food associated with America's pastime: big ol' hot dogs and salty fries. This old-fashioned red-and-white quick stop is on the west side of Main Street (adjacent to Crystal Palace). Tables spill out onto the sidewalk, where a ragtime pianist often tickles the ivories. There's a back room with a table or two, plus bleacher seating and constant screenings of sports-themed animated shorts. The bill of fare retains the mood—jumbo hot dogs, corn dog nuggets, fries, brownies, and soft drinks. You gotta love a place that supplies free cheese sauce and malt vinegar for your fries. It's a popular spot for a late-night snack, and a Magic Kingdom classic.

Crystal Palace

B L D $$–$$$ ♥

A landmark of sorts, this restaurant—one of the prettiest in the Magic Kingdom—could be a Victorian garden if not for the walls and

EARS TO YOU!

As if Mickey Mouse weren't already a sweet character, the folks at the Main Street Confectionery have made him even sweeter. Here you can get Mickey-shaped cookies, lollipops, crispie treats, candy-coated pretzels, and more. Elsewhere, you can snack on Mickey ice-cream bars. They're easy to find and colossally popular. Guests gobble up more than three million of them each year.

ceiling. The airy atmosphere provides a pleasant escape from the crowds on Main Street, and the all-you-can-eat buffet is a bountiful—if not terribly noteworthy—spread. Its main attraction is its character, make that *characters*: Winnie the Pooh and friends mingle with guests all day long.

Breakfast features a variety of hot and cold items, including omelets, fresh fruits, cereals, and such. The midday meal includes a salad bar, deli bar, pasta dishes, chicken, and fish. Dinner offers more of the same: chicken, pastas, fish, carved meats, and more. Kids love the ice-cream sundae bar (set up for lunch and dinner), as well as the pint-size and kid-appetite-appropriate section of the buffet.

Located toward the end of Main Street, U.S.A. (heading toward Adventureland), the "palace" takes its architectural cues from similar structures that once stood in New York and London's Hyde Park, and from San Francisco's Conservatory of Flowers in Golden Gate Park. There's a Victorian-style indoor flower garden, with tables that look out on flower beds, while four topiaries—Pooh, Tigger, Eeyore, and Piglet—greet guests at the entrance.

Cost for breakfast is about $19 for adults, $11 for children ages 3 through 9; lunch is about $21 for adults, $12 for children; dinner is about $31 for adults, $15 for children. Reservations are recommended.

🏃 Main Street Bakery
B L D S $ 🔴

Ever popular and always crowded, this old-fashioned bakery gives off a heavenly aroma and delivers with pastries, pies, sandwiches, and cookies. It's possible to get a quick breakfast, here, too—from bagels and breakfast sandwiches to warm cinnamon rolls. The built-to-order ice-cream cookie sandwiches and the chocolate-chunk cookies are popular indulgences. We love the frozen lattes. The nice surprise is that you can also get yogurt, granola, fresh fruit, and other dry cereal—that is, if your willpower holds out.

Hot Tip

Is the Magic Kingdom open late today? If so, consider taking the monorail or a water taxi to the Contemporary, Polynesian, Grand Floridian, or Wilderness Lodge to have an early dinner, and then return to finish the day at the Magic Kingdom. Remember to keep your ticket handy for re-entry to the park. Transportation (monorail and water taxi) generally runs for one to two hours after the park closes for the day.

🍦 Plaza Ice Cream Parlor

S | **$**

This happy place for ice-cream lovers boasts the Magic Kingdom's largest variety of hand-scooped ice-cream flavors, including no-sugar-added varieties. It's great for a before-the-parade or on-the-way-out-of-the-park nosh. To keep things moving, choose your flavors and desired number of scoops before you jump in line.

🍽 Plaza Restaurant

L D S | **$$** | 🐭

Not to be confused with the Plaza Ice Cream Parlor (above), this place also boasts ice cream as the specialty of the house. Oh, wait, that *is* confusing. Here's how to differentiate: the Ice Cream Parlor is a counter-service, cones-and-cups-only establishment. The Plaza is a table-service, you-name-a-way-to-serve-ice-cream-and-they-just-might-do-it establishment. Expect heaping sundaes, milk shakes, floats, and more. A small selection of hot and cold sandwiches, salads, and burgers are also available.

The charming atmosphere and the quality fare combine for a sweet dining experience. Reservations are recommended.

🍽 Tony's Town Square

L D | **$$$** | 🐭

Here it's possible to savor a fine view of Town Square while you bite into Italian specialties—pizzas, Caesar salad, sandwiches, and pasta. At dinnertime, the menu features chicken, grilled steaks, and spaghetti, along with a variety of daily specials. Top it off with an Italian sweet and perhaps a cup of espresso or cappuccino.

TALKIN' TURKEY

Smoked turkey legs, that is. There's something barbarically compelling about gnawing on one of these popular mega-snacks. If you've had one, you know they're pretty good. Here are some things you may not know about these giant drumsticks:

- Each one weighs about 1½ pounds.
- Disney guests gobble up more than 1½ million of them every year.
- The turkeys that once belonged to these legs weighed 40 to 50 pounds.
- They can be purchased at a cart in the Magic Kingdom's Frontierland and at the Lunching Pad at Rockettower Plaza in Tomorrowland.
- They cost about $7 a pop.

If you time it right, you can fold your napkin, pay the check, and wander out onto Main Street and enjoy the fireworks from one of the best vantage points in the Magic Kingdom. Reservations are recommended.

TOMORROWLAND

Auntie Gravity's Galactic Goodies

S **$**

Ice cream may not seem futuristic, but chances are it'll be around at least another billion years, give or take. Located across from the Tomorrowland Speedway, Auntie G's offers up smoothies, soft-serve ice cream, sundaes, and floats. There's virtually no atmosphere in this corner of the galaxy, but we still gravitate toward the goodies.

➤ Cosmic Ray's Starlight Cafe

L D S **$–$$** ❤

As big as all outdoors (not necessarily a plus), this is the largest fast-food spot in the park. Located across from Tomorrowland Indy Speedway, it's like several fast-food spots in one. There are three separate stations, with a different menu offered at each.

SPECIAL REQUESTS

Watching your salt intake? Find lactose intolerable? Most of Disney's table-service restaurants can accommodate special requirements (such as allergies to gluten or wheat, shellfish, peanuts, etc.) if requests are made at least 72 hours in advance. It's best to make your needs known when you make your advance reservations (407-WDW-DINE). Confirm your reservation and special request before arrival. Guests requiring kosher meals are encouraged to make their requests when they make their reservations. Kosher meals must be reserved at least 24 hours ahead and require a credit card (the card will not be charged unless the reservation is canceled less than 24 hours prior). **Note:** A 48-hour notice is needed for select table-service restaurants. Kosher meals are not offered at Garden View Afternoon Tea, Teppan Edo, and Tokyo Dining.

The variety is good, but you need to wait in more than one line if you want food from two or three sections. Choose from Bay 1 for rotisserie chicken, barbecue ribs, and chicken sandwiches; Bay 2 for cheeseburgers, vegetarian burgers, and hot dogs; and Bay 3 for soups, salads, chicken nuggets, sandwiches, and wraps. An Audio-Animatronics lounge singer, Sunny Eclipse, entertains all day.

Note: Cosmic Ray's Starlight Cafe offers a small number of kosher menu selections.

Lunching Pad at Rockettower Plaza

`S` `S–$$` ❤

If it's just a snack you're after, stop at the base of the Astro Orbiter for stuffed soft pretzels, frozen soda slushes, soft drinks—and even smoked turkey legs (these are substantial enough to comprise a whole meal).

Tomorrowland Terrace Noodle Station

`L D S` `S–$$` ❤

Offering pleasant views (the castle, a topiary sea serpent, graceful willow trees), this retro-futuristic spot on the edge of Tomorrowland serves noodle bowls, stir-fry selections, egg rolls, Caesar salads, chicken nuggets, and soft drinks. Operates seasonally.

Hot Tip

In the mood for a picnic? There is a small area in which to brown-bag it at the Transportation and Ticket Center (by the guest parking lot).

Epcot

The eclectic, international lineup of fare offered here threatens to over-shadow the attractions themselves. With no fewer than 11 different countries represented in the World Showcase section of the park, Epcot provides guests with the opportunity to eat their way around the world without leaving Central Florida. Less ambitious diners will likely have their taste needs met, too—there's a bountiful food court in Epcot's Future World, as well as a smattering of simple yet satiating snack spots.

FUTURE WORLD

EPCOT

🍽 Coral Reef (The Seas)

L D | **$$$** | ❤

This water-themed restaurant is all about nibbling on creatively prepared fish under the watchful eyes of their brethren. The restaurant is decorated in cool greens and blues to complement its surroundings, and every table has a panoramic view of a living coral reef; some are right up against the glass. (Don't worry: you're not actually eating Epcot residents—Disney's catches all come fresh from fishing boats in the Atlantic each day.) Menu items run the gamut from a bounty of fresh fish and shellfish, including shrimp, mahimahi, catfish, and salmon—prepared in a number of ways—to grilled New York strip steak and pan-seared chicken breast for those who are satisfied by simply spying on the fish. And save room for the "chocolate wave" dessert. Reservations are recommended.

🏃 Electric Umbrella (Innoventions Plaza)

L D S | **$–$$** | ❤

This large locale is decorated in shades of blue, mauve, and magenta. The restaurant is a good bet when the weather is temperate enough to allow dining at the tables on the terrace outside—or when bound for World Showcase with finicky eaters in tow. (There are indoor tables, too.) Offerings include burgers, chicken strips, tossed salads, and assorted sandwiches. Soft drinks and desserts are also available. Kids tend to enjoy the fare here.

HOLIDAY HOOPLA

During the Christmas holiday season, Epcot's World Showcase hosts a special Candlelight Processional. The show features a stirring choral concert and a reading of the Nativity Story by a celebrity narrator. The event is free (with park admission), but the general admission seating fills up as early as two hours before showtime. Rather than wait in line, we prefer to book a dining package—one that combines lunch or dinner at a World Showcase restaurant and guaranteed seating at the Processional. For information, call 407-934-7639. We highly recommend this package—sure, it's a luxury, but consider it an early Christmas present for yourself!

Garden Grill (The Land)
D **$$-$$$**

Guests are often so distracted by the sights and the jovial hosts (Chip, Dale, and friends) that they don't realize the restaurant is actually moving. As the restaurant revolves, and it does so quite slowly, tables drift past various dioramic scenes (which are part of the attraction Living with the Land). Among the nature scenes that may be served with dinner are a thunderstorm, sandstorm, prairie, or rainforest. The scenes were designed with diners in mind and provide you with a peek into a farmhouse window that's out of viewing range of the waterborne passengers.

Chip and Dale (who may be joined by Mickey Mouse and Pluto) host the character meal here each day. The menu features rotisserie meats, fresh vegetables (some of which are grown inside The Land pavilion), and a small selection of desserts. There is a separate kids' menu. For adults, the cost is about $29. Kids pay $14. Beverages and dessert (you can decorate your own cupcake) are included. Meals are served family style (unlimited, communal platters for the table). Reservations are recommended.

The restaurant moves in a circle. It's imperceptible to most, but if you are highly sensitive to motion it may be best to dine in a more stationary environment.

🏃 Sunshine Seasons (The Land)

B L D S **S–$$** 🐭

It's the closest thing to a mall food court you'll find in a Walt Disney World park, but a bit more hectic. Located near the entrance to Soarin' on the pavilion's lower level, this is an ideal destination for parties who can't quite agree on any one type of fare—there's bound to be something for everyone. Tables are scattered in several areas, beneath colorful hot-air balloons. Scouting out a table can be a challenge during peak mealtimes. (There's also quite a bit of pedestrian congestion, thanks to the enormous popularity of Soarin'.)

The Sandwich Shop offers a variety of sandwiches, including ham and salami grinders, and a roasted vegetable Cuban sandwich. **The Bakery**'s desserts include candy-bar cheesecake, brownies, and ice-cream bars. There is also a "grab and go" section for guests in a hurry. Among the

items to choose from are sushi, fruit and cheese plates, salads, and snack foods. **Grill Shop** offers rotisserie chicken, grilled salmon, and pork chops. **The Soup & Salad Shop** serves the likes of roasted beet and goat cheese salads and seared tuna salad with sesame rice wine dressing. There is a selection of soups, too. Finally, the **Wok Shop** has Mongolian beef with jasmine rice and noodle bowls (including one of the vegetarian variety).

A word of advice: It's a good idea to split up your party and stand in several lines at once. That'll increase your chances of actually eating together. Before you do so, select a table. That way, everyone in the party will know where to meet after they forage.

Hot Tip

The "Wine & Dine" plan may be added to any meal-inclusive package. It includes a bottle of wine per night, per room from a designated wine list. One entitlement may be used for select bottles of vino. Wines by the glass and half bottles are not included.

WORLD SHOWCASE

📷🍽 Akershus Royal Banquet Hall (Norway)

B L D $$-$$$ 🐭

At Epcot's castlelike Akershus, guests are treated to authentic Norwegian cuisine. This is your chance to sample well-prepared signature dishes that rarely make their way into theme parks. Try a sampling of the Norwegian *koldtbord*, a buffet featuring smoked salmon and seafood, authentic Norwegian cheeses, and chilled salads, followed by one of the ever-changing line-ups of Norwegian-inspired entrées, including seafood, beef, and poultry selections. The kids' menu offers grilled chicken, ravioli, pasta with meatballs, and hot dogs. Dessert is included, as are soft drinks. Don't be daunted by the odd-sounding names of some dishes; servers will explain the offerings.

Princess Storybook dining takes place here daily (breakfast, lunch, and dinner). It's an excellent alternative to Cinderella's Royal Table (which is very difficult to reserve). While guests enjoy the all-you-can-eat fare, Disney princesses wander about and mingle. Belle, Jasmine, Snow White, Sleeping Beauty, and even Mulan have made appearances. Guests get a special souvenir at meal's end—a complimentary set of photos with one of the Disney princesses! (Each set includes one 6-by-8-inch print and four 4-by-6-inch prints and is presented in a themed folder.) Note that the character appearance schedule varies. Reservations must be made with a credit card. Changes and cancellations must be made at least 48 hours ahead to avoid a $10 per person charge.

Biergarten (Germany)
L D **$$–$$$** ♥

Year in and year out, this place makes us happy. It's a reasonably priced, all-you-can-eat buffet of traditional German cuisine set in a charming courtyard. Adding to the fun are communal tables and live entertainment (at lunch and dinner). It's pretty much Oktoberfest year-round.

The hearty, varied buffet features a selection of sausages, rotisserie chicken, spaetzle, chicken schnitzel, potato salad, cucumber salad, and many other German specialties. Wash it all down with soft drinks, German wine, or a stein of beer (suds purists may grouse at the limited selection of beer). Among the dessert options is apple strudel with vanilla sauce.

The entertainment consists of occasional appearances by traditional Bavarian musicians—each clad in lederhosen or dirndl—who play accordions, cowbells, a musical saw, and a harplike stringed instrument known as the "wooden laughter." Performances take place at scheduled times in the dining room. Diners are usually invited to join the fun on the dance floor. Because entertainment is intermittent, there's plenty of time to enjoy the pleasant setting. Reservations are recommended, particularly during peak seasons.

Bistro de Paris (France)
D **$$$$**

This intimate bistro—one flight above Chefs de France—puts on romantic airs rather than the usual bustle. The elegant decor, with its evocative interplay of brass sconces, milk-glass chandeliers, mirrors, and leaded glass, is convincingly French. And, if you're one of the lucky few who arrive as a window-side table opens up, you'll be treated to a rather unique view of World Showcase.

The traditional upscale bistro menu (created by the same chefs responsible for the menu at Chefs de France; see page 41) features such robust "preludes" as a medley of escargot, frog legs, and *foie gras*. The entrée menu includes a veal chop, beef tenderloin, and Maine lobster. This is hearty dining, so you might want to stroll around the promenade to walk off your meal—and your chocolate soufflé. The impressive wine list is *très* French. Reservations are recommended.

Boulangerie Patisserie (France)

L D S $-$$

For some, a visit to Epcot is incomplete without stopping by this ever-popular pastry shop, tucked toward the back of the France pavilion. Crowds are forever lining up to consume the flaky croissants, éclairs, fruit tarts, and chocolate mousse. (We swear by the napoleons.) It's also possible to indulge in a cheese plate, a ham and cheese quiche, or a ham and cheese croissant. The baguettes are *magnifique*. Wash it all down with espresso, cappuccino, or hot chocolate.

The treats were selected under the management of the chefs who were the culinary brains behind the Chefs de France restaurant not far away. This has become a favorite snacking stop among Epcot veterans. Your best bet is to stop here as soon as World Showcase opens or during IllumiNations, the nightly fireworks show (though you can't see the show from here).

JUST FOR GOLFERS

If you plan on playing on the Osprey Ridge course, keep in mind that Disney's Osprey Ridge Golf Club has a pleasant dining option just for you. It's called Sand Trap Bar & Grill (🐾), and it's open for three meals a day.

Cantina de San Angel (Mexico)

L D S **$–$$** 🐾

Located along the World Showcase Promenade, just outside the entrance to Mexico's pyramid, this stand serves burritos, tacos al carbón, flour tortillas filled with grilled chicken strips, onions, and peppers (served with refried beans and salsa), and churros (fried dough rolled in cinnamon and sugar). Beer and margaritas are available.

Chefs de France (France)

L D **$$$–$$$$** 🐾

"Bright lights, big dining room" describes this airy establishment. With some of France's best chefs responsible for this nouvelle French kitchen, the results are rewarding. The menu features fresh ingredients readily available from Florida purveyors, though the restaurant imports as many key ingredients from France as possible.

The offerings are French, but the foundation of the menu is nouvelle cuisine, which involves lighter sauces using less cream and butter than in classic French cooking. Menu items include seared tuna, and lamb and beef filets. Soups and appetizers, such as onion soup and escargot, are all-day staples.

Chocolate tarts and crème brûlée are dessert specialties. Wine pairings are recommended from a modest (though well-rounded) list.

This is one of the most expensive of all World Showcase restaurants. Still, given its popularity, many guests believe it's worth the splurge. Reservations are a must.

🏃 Cool Post
(between Germany and China)
S **$**

As its name suggests, this place specializes in all things cool: ice cream, beer, and soft drinks. Located between the Germany and China pavilions, it may offer a refreshing spritz of water when the weather is warm.

🏃 Yorkshire County Fish Shop
(United Kingdom)
L D S **$** 🍴

A perfect choice for a quick snack or a light lunch, this stand offers scrumptious fish and chips. (Don't forget the malt vinegar.) Cola, iced tea, light lemonade, bottled water, coffee, and Bass Ale are also available.

🏃 Kringla Bakeri og Kafe
(Norway)
L D S **$-$$** 🍴

This small bake shop serves *kringles,* sweet pretzels reserved for special occasions in Norway; *vaflers,* heart-shaped waffles topped with powdered sugar and jam; *lefse*, potato bread with cinnamon sugar; and sandwiches such as smoked salmon, roast beef, or ham and cheese. There are no seats inside the bakery, but you can eat in the small, shaded outdoor eating area.

🍽 Le Cellier Steakhouse (Canada)

L D **$$–$$$** 🐭

We love retreating to this peaceful wine cellar-like spot, a favorite place for a hearty meal. It may seem a bit dungeony to some critics, but we like that; you really feel as though you're inside a wine cellar. The restaurant has low ceilings, lantern light, and stone walls, all of which contribute to the atmosphere.

There's a full menu of tempting Canadian foods, starting with a bread basket that

FOOD AND WINE FESTIVAL

Once a year, Epcot's already-hopping dining scene expands exponentially in what's known as the International Food and Wine Festival. The event, which usually runs from late September through early November, is a celebration of the flavors of dozens of nations. Those countries without permanent stations at World Showcase set up temporary displays from which authentic samples of food and wine are sold. The samples generally range in price from about $2 to about $8. It's possible to eat and drink your way around the world for about the same price as some table-service restaurants.

The festival also features demonstrations from top chefs, as well as wine and cooking seminars. For specifics, visit *www.disneyworld.com* or call 407-824-4321.

includes a pretzel, plus sourdough, and whole-grain creations. At both lunch and dinner, the cheddar cheese soup is a hit (it's been on the menu since Le Cellier opened). Midday, there's a steak salad or prime rib sandwich. Specialties such as pan-seared salmon and filet mignon are on both the lunch and dinner menus, along with chicken, pasta, and pork dishes. For dessert, try the crème brûlée or chocolate cake. Microbrews from Quebec, Canadian lagers, and Inniskillin and Mission Hill wines are served. Reservations are recommended.

🏃 Liberty Inn (The American Adventure)
L D S $-$$ 🏵

While it may seem like the flavors of the United States get short shrift when it comes to representation at Epcot, that's not the case here. True, there's no America-oriented table-service restaurant at World Showcase, though the Garden Grill over in Future World proudly serves up platters of Americana. On the international side of the park, Liberty Inn dishes out what many think of as American food: burgers, hot dogs, and fries. Also on the menu are chicken nuggets, chicken Caesar salads, chicken sand-wiches, and desserts (think fruit cups and apple cobbler). Located on the left side of the American Adventure pavilion, this is a good choice for children and picky eaters.

🏃 Lotus Blossom Cafe (China)
L D S $-$$ 🏵

The fare may not live up to the splendor of the rest of this pavilion, but if you crave a quick Chinese food fix, this place, adjacent to the shopping gallery in the China pavilion, offers orange chicken, Mongolian-style beef sandwiches, salad, egg rolls, pot stickers, spinach beef noodle soup, and more. There is a covered outdoor seating area nearby.

Marrakesh (Morocco)
L D S $$–$$$ ❤

It's not every day that you can slip into an exquisitely tiled Moroccan palace and expect to be entertained by belly dancers and musicians as you polish off a plate of Moroccan cuisine; even the waiters are dressed in traditional costumes. Want to know how authentic this place is? The king of Morocco sent craftspeople to Epcot to make sure they were creating a real Moroccan atmosphere. (Unfortunately, the fare plays second fiddle to the surroundings.) Specialties include roast lamb, chicken brochette, beef shish kebab, and couscous. Want to experience all of it? Sampler platters are available. Reservations are recommended, but it's often possible to get in without much of a wait.

Mitsukoshi (Japan)
L D $$$ ❤

Within the sprawling Mitsukoshi complex (which is named for and run by the Japanese company of the same name), there are two options:

Tokyo Dining occupies a chic, colorful space in the Mitsukoshi building. If you're in the mood for sushi, sashimi, or tempura (batter-dipped, deep-fried chicken, beef, seafood, and vegetables), grilled chicken, salmon, or New York strip steak, head here. It's also possible to munch on *edamame* (steamed soybeans) and indulge in sake and

FUN WiTH FOOD

Remember when squishing gooey peanut butter through your fingers was a delightfully visceral experience? Well, throw in some marshmallows and chocolate sprinkles, and you have a dessert fit for a king—or, at least, for a kid. It's not as gross as it sounds. In fact, this creative confection is one of the most popular of the "interactive desserts" that grace the menus of many Walt Disney World restaurants.

Another example: young diners at Epcot's Le Cellier Steakhouse have changed chocolate mousse into "moose" by adding faces and antlers. Note that interactive desserts aren't offered everywhere and are subject to change.

Japanese beer, among other drinks. Reservations are recommended.

Teppan Edo, Tokyo Dining's lively neighbor, fills the space formerly occupied by Teppanyaki Dining Room. As with its predecessor, guests here sit around a large *teppan* grill and watch as a nimble chef demonstrates just how quickly enough chicken, beef, seafood, and vegetables to feed eight people can be chopped, seasoned, and stir-fried. Entrées are sizzling and satisfying. Soups, salads, sushi, desserts, and cocktails (including Japanese beer and sake) are also on the menu. Don't wear your finest attire: There's always the potential for a little splattering here and there. Reservations are recommended.

 Nine Dragons (China)
LD **$$$** 🍴

This stop on Epcot's varied international restaurant tour offers family-style meals prepared in provincial Chinese cooking styles. On the appetizer menu, expect to find items such as lightly spiced cucumber salad, shrimp summer rolls, and chicken dumplings. Entrées include everything from sweet-and-sour pork to the spicy Kung Pao chicken, vegetable stir fry, five-spiced fish, and a peppery shrimp with spinach noodles.

A nice variety of imported Chinese teas, beers, and wines is available. Dessert selections include red-bean ice cream, ginger ice cream, and the house-baked ginger tiramisu. Reservations are recommended.

Refreshment Port (Canada)
S **$**

A good spot for a quick thirst-quencher and a snack on the go. Located on the World Showcase Promenade, this stand serves fries, chicken nuggets, frozen desserts, and soft drinks (soda, juice, milk, coffee, etc.).

Hot Tip

That gift card burning a hole in your pocket? The Walt Disney World Shopping and Dining Gift Card may be redeemed at all Disney-owned-and-operated dining, shopping, and recreation locations where credit cards are accepted. If you lose track of what's left on your card, simply call the number on the back to find out.

Rose & Crown Pub & Dining Room (United Kingdom)

L D S **$$–$$$** 🐭

Don't let the word "pub" throw you. While this place serves up what is arguably some of the best brews on Walt Disney World property, its dining area is also known for such crowd-pleasing dishes as crispy fish and chips, grilled steaks, and bangers and mash (sausages with mashed potatoes).

Dessert options include, among other things, sticky toffee pudding and warm apple crumble topped with ice cream. Bass Ale from England and Harp Lager and Guinness Stout, both from Ireland, are on tap. (They're served cold, in the American fashion, not at room temperature, as some Brits prefer.)

The atmosphere is welcoming. It incorporates several architectural styles from the 18th and 19th centuries, which add up to a believable, enjoyable re-creation of the charming pubs so common in the English countryside. In fine weather it's pleasant to lunch under a canopy on the terrace outside and watch the *FriendShip* water taxis cruising across World Showcase Lagoon.

The pub section of the Rose & Crown serves such snacks as a fruit and cheese plate and fish and chips—along with all the brews noted above and traditional British mixed drinks, such as shandies (Bass Ale and Sprite), lager with lime juice, and black and tans (Bass Ale and Guinness Stout). This spot is quite popular, so it's often necessary to queue up at the door. But the wait is seldom very long, since few guests choose to linger over their drinks. A piano player is sometimes on hand to entertain revelers. Note that the pub section also spills out onto the promenade—where the first-come, first-snagged waterside tables make for a nice spot to sip a drink and, possibly, enjoy a snack from a nearby stand. Reservations are not available in the pub areas, but are highly recommended for the adjacent restaurant.

🍽 San Angel Inn (Mexico)
LD **$$$** 🐭

The lights are low, the mood is romantic, and there is a smoking volcano poised tableside. If that's not enchantment enough, there's a mystical pyramid and a moonlit river. It all takes place inside the pyramid that serves as the Mexico pavilion. (To get there, you'll have to meander through the marketplace known as La Plaza de los Amigos.)

The menu? You'll find Mexican fare from margaritas to chicken molé. And there's more: The eatery also offers a variety of more subtly flavored fish, poultry, and meat dishes. To start, there's *coctel de camarones* (shrimp coctail with tomato juice, peppers, onions, cilantro, and avocado), soups, and salads.

For entrées, the menu offers grilled tenderloin of beef with poblano peppers and fried plantains, crispy shrimp over cold potato salad, roast duck breast, and mahimahi with an aromatic sauce of olives, bell peppers, onions, tomatoes, and white wine. Mexican desserts may be unfamiliar to many North Americans, with the possible exception of the custard known as flan, but are well worth trying. Dos Equis beer and margaritas make good accompaniments. Reservations are recommended. Note that some dishes may have a little kick. Ask your server if you're concerned. She or he can steer you toward less spicy selections. If you crave more heat, you'll have to supply it yourself—they don't have hot sauce.

🏃 Sommerfest (Germany)
L D S **$–$$** 🐭

Here, speedy sustenance takes such classic forms as bratwurst, frankfurters, and soft pretzels (if they're too dry, we send them back). For dessert, there's Black Forest cake and apple strudel. The shaded outdoor seating area sports a festive mural. German wine and Becks and Franziskaner Weisse beer are offered at this establishment, located toward the rear of the pavilion.

🏃 Tangierine Cafe (Morocco)
L D S **$–$$** 🐭

Named for the Moroccan city of Tangier, this casual spot serves (unremarkable) Mediterranean specialties—lentil salad, hummus, and tabbouleh, as well as rotisserie chicken and lamb presented as sandwiches (served on Moroccan bread), and combination platters (including one designed with vegetarians in mind). Specialty coffees and pastries are available.

🍽 Tutta Italia (Italy)
L D S **$$–$$$** 🐭

There's a new menu at one of the most popular World Showcase restaurants, and the addition of outdoor tables makes it one of the more pleasant spots for dining at Epcot (when the weather cooperates, that is). Traditional starters such as fried calamari, fresh mozzarella with tomatoes and basil, and Caesar salad can make a meal in and of themselves. However, we recommend sampling the fresh pastas—made here daily—spaghetti, tagliatelle, lasagna, and more. Kids like the sachetti (pasta pillows filled with ricotta and mozzarella served with a simple tomato sauce). Fish, pork, and chicken entrées round out the menu. At lunchtime, paninis are also an option. Dessert lovers should save room for the cannoli, mocha tiramisu, gelati (Italian ice cream), or sorbet. The dining room may be renovated in the not-too-distant future, but the already refurbished menu is worth considering now.

✈ Yakitori House (Japan)

L D S | **$** | ✿

Easy to miss, what with its out-of-the-way location, this is an ideal spot to go to escape the masses and savor a simple, relaxing meal. To get there, you'll need to find the path to the left of the Japan pavilion. The path deposits you in a peaceful Japanese garden. The no-frills restaurant sits to the right of the garden. The fare here includes *guydon* (a stewlike concoction flavored with soy sauce), *edamame* (steamed soybeans), sushi rolls, teriyaki chicken, and Japanese sweets (desserts include chestnut cake). Drinks extend to green tea, Kirin beer, and sake (rice wine served hot or cold).

Hot Tip

If you plan to see IllumiNations, know that the show takes place nightly at 9 P.M. Try to time it so your evening meal winds up no later than 8:45 P.M. —and tell your server when you arrive.

Hot Tip

The Disney Dining Plan does not include gratuity. Please don't forget to tip your servers at table-service eateries. Figure on about 18–20 percent (for good service).

CHECK, PLEASE!

Paying for a meal at Disney World is a piece of cake—especially if you have a Disney resort ID (and back it up with a major credit card upon check-in). Resort IDs are accepted by most restaurants on WDW property. Notable exceptions: eateries at the Swan and Dolphin resorts, some Downtown Disney spots, Hotel Plaza Boulevard resorts, and some snack carts. Simply hand it to the waiter or cashier, sign the bill (don't forget to add a tip where appropriate), and the charge will appear on your hotel statement at check-out.

Of course, there are other ways to pay the piper. In addition to U.S. currency, which is welcome everywhere, traveler's checks and major credit cards are accepted in most non-cart locations. Foreign currency is a no-no. Disney currency (aka Disney Dollars) works like cash in all Disney-owned-and-operated venues. Disney Gift Cards are accepted at most WDW owned-and-operated establishments. (If you plan to pay with a gift card, tell your server when you place your order.)

Disney's Hollywood Studios

Lights, camera, lunch! This theme park, designed to resemble a working Hollywood backlot circa the 1940s, tackles the role of feeding guests with style and whimsy. Here you can sit in a classic car and enjoy a meal at a drive-in, rub elbows with the beautiful people at a reproduction of the Hollywood Brown Derby, and play the part of sitcom kid as you're served by "Mom" or "Dad" at the 50's Prime Time Cafe (no elbows on the table, please!). While the attention to theming is obvious, it doesn't upstage the fare. So grab a napkin, and get ready for your close-up.

 ABC Commissary
B L D S **$–$$** 🔴

Located near the Chinese Theater, this spot
has shaken up the menu a few times of late.
Most recently, it featured fish and chips,
cheeseburgers, chicken curry, and Cuban
sandwiches. Dessert items include strawberry
parfait and chocolate mousse. For breakfast,
think danish, cereal, fruit, and sandwiches.
Soft drinks and beer are served. The restaurant is huge and does indeed resemble an
actual studio commissary. We could do without the ads for ABC shows, which play on a
continuous loop from TVs scattered throughout the dining area. Enough already!

Backlot Express
L D S **$–$$** 🔴

Designed to look like a crafts shop on an old
studio backlot, this eatery is near the Star
Tours attraction. The indoor seating areas
carry out the prop-shop theme, with paint-
speckled floors, car engines, and various
other spare prop parts. The outdoor tables are
situated amid plants and trees. Menu offerings include burgers, chicken strips, hot dogs,
grilled turkey and cheese sandwiches, grilled
veggie sandwiches, and salads. For dessert,
there's marble cheesecake and strawberry
parfait. Soft drinks and beer are available.

The Dip Site
S **$**

A tiny tin shack, which sits beside the
Indiana Jones Epic Stunt Spectacular, the
Dip Site dispenses chips, popcorn, frozen
lemonade, water, and beer.

FANTASMIC! DINNER PACKAGE

Guests who make dining arrangements at their Disney resort or at any of the parks can take advantage of the Fantasmic! Dining Opportunity Special. Reserved seating for the evening's performance of Fantasmic! comes with the meal at no extra cost.

Why book the package? Besides guaranteeing a seat for dinner, it ensures that you will get seating for Fantasmic! without having to wait in line. This is critical—since guests start lining up for the show as much as two hours ahead. With the package, you can have a relaxing dinner and head over to the show shortly before it starts.

Call 407-939-3463 for more information or to book a "dinner and a show" package. At press time, the Hollywood Brown Derby, Hollywood & Vine, and Mama Melrose's Ristorante Italiano were participating in the program. (Even though the Fantasmic! Dining Opportunity *may* be available for walk-ups, we highly recommend booking it in advance—you've got nothing to lose.)

50's Prime Time Cafe

L D $$–$$$

This retreat to the era of *I Love Lucy* is an amusing amalgam of comfort food, kitschy 1950s-style kitchen nooks, and attentive servers of the "No talking with your mouth full" ilk. Nostalgia abounds, with more cookie jars than you could shake an Oreo at, all meant to bring you back to childhood of yesteryear; even the dessert menu is read on an old ViewMaster, and TVs broadcast black-and-white clips from favorite fifties comedies (all related to food). Guests are waited on by "Mom" (and other family members) with considerable enthusiasm: They make recommendations and encourage everyone to keep their elbows off the table, eat their vegetables, and clean their plates (or no dessert!). Misbehave and you may have to stand in the corner (the 1950s version of a "time out").

Adding to the appeal is the menu, which is packed with comfort foods. For openers, there's a choice of homemade chicken noodle soup or onion rings. Specialties of the house include magnificent meat loaf, served with mashed potatoes and vegetables; fried chicken; and old-fashioned pot roast. There are Caesar salads, sandwiches, and chicken pot pie, too. Milk shakes, ice-cream sodas, and root beer floats are filling accompaniments. And when you've finished everything on your plate, "Mom" will ask if you'd like dessert. Standouts include s'mores—graham crackers topped with chocolate and toasted marshmallows (you'll feel like you're at summer camp)—sundaes, seasonal cobbler, and angel food cake with berries and whipped cream. A full bar is available. Kids of all ages love this place. Reservations are recommended.

BABY NEEDS

Babies. They're a needy lot. Fortunately, most of the requisite supplies can be found somewhere at Disney World—if you know where to look. Formula and jarred food can be purchased at the Baby Care Center in each of the theme parks and at every WDW resort. Most restaurants have kids' menus with toddler-friendly food (mac and cheese, chicken nuggets, and the like).

If your baby is partial to a specific formula or brand of food, consider shipping a box of it to your hotel before you leave home. Keep in mind that there are several grocery stores near Disney World. If you'll have a car, it may be worth the trip (a guest relations clerk can offer directions). The selections are more varied, as are the prices. Stash perishables in an in-room refrigerator—they rent for about $10 per night in WDW "value" resorts and are free in the "deluxe" and "moderate" resorts. It's best to request one when you make your reservation. Some other points of interest regarding baby diners at WDW:

• Most eateries have high chairs and booster seats. Request one when you make your restaurant reservation.
• Stroller use inside restaurants is discouraged. Park it outside.

Continued on page 58

• WDW restaurants are often chilly. Be sure to pack a sweater or blanket.

• Be it a fast-food or table-service restaurant, bring toys to keep the little one(s) busy.

• The following resorts have 24-hour snack bars: Grand Floridian, Dolphin, Polynesian, Regal Sun, and Buena Vista Palace (on Hotel Plaza Boulevard). The middle-of-the-night pickin's may be slim, but milk and cereal are served 'round the clock.

• If you'd like a quiet spot to nurse an infant, head to a Baby Care Center in any of the theme parks. They all have rooms with rocking chairs.

• If you're headed for a long day in a theme park, pack simple, healthy snacks for toddlers.

• To make your dining experience less harried, consider feeding your baby before you get to the restaurant.

Hollywood & Vine
B L D **$$$**

The exterior is Art Deco, and the interior conjures up memories of a 1950s American diner—forged out of stainless steel with pink accents. It's next door to the 50's Prime Time Cafe, just off Hollywood Boulevard.

The buffet breakfast and lunch, known as Playhouse Disney's Play 'n Dine, are character affairs featuring Jo Jo and Goliath from *Jo Jo's Circus* and Leo from *The Little*

Hot Tip

If you can stand to miss the evening's performance of Fantasmic! (Disney's Hollywood Studios nighttime spectacular), consider dining in one of the park's popular eateries during the show.

Einsteins. The morning meal includes Mickey waffles, frittatas, fresh fruits, and "house-made" pastries. Lunch may offer items such as herb-crusted baked salmon with citrus butter, multigrain pasta with red pepper pesto, and salads. Dinner, which is character-free, also features carved meats, peel-and-eat shrimp, and mussels. Some soft drinks are included. Beer and wine are served at an extra cost. Reservations are recommended.

Hollywood Brown Derby
L D $$–$$$

The Studios' most gracious dining is found at this faithful revival of the original *cause célèbre*, which opened on Hollywood and Vine in 1926. Dressed to the nines in chandeliers and celebrity caricatures, the restaurant stokes the appetite with its ever-so-finely chopped signature Cobb salad (invented by Brown Derby owner Bob Cobb) and grapefruit cake—a Brown Derby institution. Some of the fare is a bit highbrow (and high-priced) for the theme park crowd, but if you're up for a splurge, this spot is sure to rise to the occasion. We recommend the fresh seared ahi tuna; steaks get good marks, too.

The slightly formal atmosphere is not likely to enchant most kids, but youngster-friendly fare is available. The New World wine list is excellent. Reservations are recommended.

Mama Melrose's Ristorante Italiano

L D **$$–$$$** ❤

This pleasant Italian restaurant (with a California twist) is located in a large warehouse that has been converted into a dining room. Flatbreads are prepared in a wood-burning oven. The menu also features grilled fish, pasta, and vegetarian options. Dishes include spaghetti with clams and mussels in a spicy marinara sauce, and spicy Italian sausage. If you like fish, you may enjoy the salmon; it rates high with us. The wine list includes selections from California and Italy. Reservations are recommended.

Min and Bill's Dockside Diner

S **$**

Mmm . . . milk shakes. 'Nuf said. In addition to some of the greatest, thickest chocolate and vanilla shakes in the World, Min and Bill's waterside snack spot also serves cookies, pretzels stuffed with cheese or apple, coffee, soft drinks, and beer. To find it, look for the boat with the line to board, er, buy.

FYI: *Min and Bill* was a 1930s feature film (one of the first talkies) that took place on a waterfront. Hence, the lakefront locale.

Pizza Planet

L D S **$–$$** ❤

Located inside a kid-magnet arcade, this is a counter-service spot with a limited but youngster-friendly menu. Select from simple individual pizzas, salads, cookies, apple slices, Mickey crispie treats, and soft drinks (including milk and apple juice). There is outdoor seating.

Hot Tip

While the Sci-Fi Dine-In Theater has tables that can accommodate guests who use wheelchairs, there aren't many. Be sure to request such a table when you make your reservations—and confirm it by phone before you go; 407-WDW-DINE (939-3463).

Sci-Fi Dine-In Theater
L D **$$–$$$**

A convincing re-creation of a drive-in theater, the atmosphere here is completely absorbing. The tables are actually flashy, 1950s-era cars, complete with fins and whitewalls. Stars twinkle overhead in the "night sky," and drive-in theater speakers are mounted beside each car. Most seats are within cars, with most featuring front- and backseat counters facing front. Not terribly conducive to meaningful table talk, but ideal for viewing the large movie screen, where a 45-minute compilation of the best (and worst) of science-fiction trailers and cartoons plays in a continuous loop. There are a couple of traditional tables within oversize cars—if this is your preference, make that known when you book the table and expect to wait a bit when you arrive.

Selections include Reuben sandwiches, chicken sandwiches, barbecue ribs, and shrimp pasta. Kids enjoy the Mickey-plate pizza. The slate of desserts includes cheesecake, milk shakes, and ice-cream sundaes. It's a bit expensive, but the "show" aspect is worth it to many. It's popular with all ages. There are a few tables that accommodate guests using wheelchairs. Reservations are recommended.

🏃 Starring Rolls Cafe

B L S $-$$ 💟

In a hurry? Here's where you can get the day off to a quick start, or take a cookie or a coffee break. Rolls, pastries, muffins, croissants, and no-sugar-added desserts are sold at this sweet-smelling shop. Coffee (beans are ground on-site), tea, and soft drinks are also served. For lunch, sandwiches and wine are available.

🏃 Studio Catering Co.

L D S $-$$ 💟

Next to the Honey, I Shrunk the Kids Movie Set Adventure, this spot offers grilled chicken with black beans and rice, pulled pork sandwiches, and more. There is a full bar serving specialty libations, too.

🏃 Sunset Ranch Market

L D S $-$$ 💟

A celebration of California's outdoor lifestyle, this open-air cluster of snack stands has something for everyone. **Rosie's All-American Cafe** sells cheeseburgers, veggie burgers, chicken nuggets, salads, and soups. **Catalina Eddie's** offers plain and pepperoni pizzas, hot Italian deli-style sandwiches, salads, chocolate-fudge cake, and carrot cake. Fruit, carrots, pretzels, granola bars, pickles, and soft drinks are available at **Anaheim Produce**. **Toluca Legs Turkey Co.** serves (enormous) turkey legs and salads, barbecued pulled-pork subs, chili, hot dogs, and chips. **Hollywood Scoops Ice Cream** offers creamy treats (including sugar-free vanilla). **Fairfax Fries** serves french fries and soft drinks.

Disney's Animal Kingdom

Walt Disney World's nature-oriented theme park is ideal for grazers: with more than a dozen spots to nosh, it may not be strong on table-service (there are three such eateries), but it takes "quick service" quite seriously. When your stomach starts growling like the beasts at the Kilimanjaro Safaris attraction, consider the top-notch Tusker House and Flame Tree Barbecue. Not only do they offer mouth-watering meals, but they serve them in some of the fanciest theme park dining environments around.

63

Anandapur Ice Cream Truck

`S` `$`

This ice-cream truck doesn't actually move, but the Asia-based vehicle does deliver chilly treats. Ice cream is available by the cone or in a soda float.

Dino Bite Snacks

`S` `$` 🐭

In DinoLand, U.S.A., on the far side of Chester and Hester's DinoRama, is a small stand that offers desserts throughout the day. We recently got yogurt here, too.

Flame Tree Barbecue

`L D S` `$-$$` 🐭

If you can't find this eatery, just follow your nose. Because when the kitchen is cooking, the scent is compelling. It serves up a selection of barbecued sandwiches and platters, all wood roasted. Sample the mild, tomato-based barbecue sauce or the spicy, mustard-based Carolina-style sauce with your smoked beef brisket, pulled pork, or hickory-smoked St. Louis ribs. (Disney's ovens produce 1,200 pounds at a time. Want the recipe? Just ask.) Smoked turkey sandwiches, salads, and key lime pie round out the options.

Picnic in the Park

Picnic-style meals are offered at Animal Kingdom. Order yours (for a party of 3 to 6) at the Picnic in the Park podium near Guest Relations or at Tusker House. For details, call 407-WDW-DINE. 🐭

ANIMAL KINGDOM

There's outdoor seating along the river (which is quite lovely when it's not 98 degrees). If Flame Tree isn't serving, the tables are still open for use. It's located on Discovery Island, near DinoLand.

🏃 Harambe Fruit Market

`S` `$`

Sometimes, a crunchy apple is just what the doctor—or the hungry theme park guest—ordered. Apples, among other healthy snacks, are available at this fruit stand near the entrance to Kilimanjaro Safaris. Water and sports drinks are sold here, too.

🏃 Kusafiri Coffee Shop & Bakery

`B S` `$`

The bakery next to Tusker House provides a steady stream of breakfast treats and assorted desserts, plus cappuccino and espresso.

🏃 Pizzafari

`L D S` `$-$$` 🐭

This big, colorful dining area has no-nonsense fare that tends to please young palates. Salads and hot Italian-style sand-wiches are also on the menu. Animal murals decorate the walls of this restaurant, located on Discovery Island, near the bridge to Camp Minnie-Mickey.

🍽 Rainforest Cafe

`B L D S` `$$-$$$`

Animal Kingdom's original table-service restaurant is located at its front entrance.

The atmosphere blends well with the theme park it borders. Environmentally conscious cuisine includes items like Planet Earth Pasta and the Plant Sandwich. (The Calypso Dip—fresh salmon, artichoke hearts, onions, spices, and cheese served with warm pita—is consistently yummy.) There's no net-caught fish on the menu nor beef from countries that destroy rainforest land to raise cattle. Fish tanks, tropical decor, and the occasional thunderstorm add to the ambience (and noise level). Kids thrive here.

The restaurant and bar are accessible from inside and outside Animal Kingdom, so admission to the park isn't necessary to enter. (There is another location at Downtown Disney Marketplace.) Reservations are recommended for all meals.

Restaurantosaurus
L D S **$-$$** ❤

Hang a right once you enter DinoLand, U.S.A., and you'll discover this spot. Themed as a campsite for student paleontologists, this eatery is filled with fossils, with class notes lining the walls. The kitchen offers fast food at lunch and dinner: burgers, chicken salad, and hot dogs—plus french fries, chicken nuggets, and kids' meals.

Royal Anandapur Tea Co.
S **$**

After hiking through Africa to get to Asia, guests can build up quite a thirst. That's where this exotic tea stand comes in handy. Located near the Yak & Yeti, stop here for a variety of iced and hot teas, fruit smoothies, specialty coffees, and sweet treats.

WATER PARK DINING

Disney's duo of water parks, Typhoon Lagoon and Blizzard Beach, provides plenty of opportunities to defy Mom's plea to wait an hour to splash after you nosh. The fare is limited to the quick-service kind (who wants a sit-down meal in a soggy swimsuit?) and what it lacks in creativity, it makes up for in convenience and appeal: Burgers, hot dogs, pizzas, salads, ice cream, and snacks are sold at spots with names like Typhoon Tilly's (🐭), Leaning Palms (🐭), and Avalunch (🐭). Frozen drink specialties flow at Let's Go Slurpin' (Typhoon Lagoon) and at Blizzard Beach's Polar Bear Pool Bar.

Some folks take the day-at-the-beach theme seriously enough to pack a picnic lunch. Coolers may be brought into both parks, but alcoholic beverages and glass containers may not.

Tamu Tamu Refreshments
S **$**

This walk-up window dispenses burgers and shakes. There's a small seating nook next door. It's in Harambe, just across the way from Tusker House.

Tusker House
B L D S **$–$$** 🐭

The Tusker House fare—which is now offered buffet-style—is head, shoulders, and antlers above the rest. We dig the carved chairs inside, but somehow the Safari Amber beer tastes better outside (there are outdoor tables). It's on the left side of Harambe, just over the bridge from Discovery Island. Donald Duck fans are especially pleased with the addition of Donald's Safari Breakfast buffet. It's offered daily and includes visits from the aforementioned fowl, plus Mickey, Daisy, and Goofy. Breakfast hours run from 8 A.M. until 10:30 A.M., while lunch and dinner are offered from 11:30 A.M. till park closing time. The Kusafiri Coffee Shop & Bakery operates from a window outside.

Yak & Yeti

L D S $$-$$$ 🐭

Grab a set of chopsticks and dig in! This elaborate venue is a much-welcome addition to the small Animal Kingdom family of table-service eateries (It opened for business in 2008). Nestled deep in the park's village of Anandapur (across from the entrance to Kali River Rapids), the restaurant—which opens at 10 A.M.—specializes in Asian-fusion cuisine. Its shop offers goods ranging from sushi plates to fine teapots. There is a quick-service area nearby. It serves lunch and dinner.

Hot Tip

Do you have a WDW Annual Pass? If so, know that many Disney World eateries offer lunchtime discounts for you and up to three guests. Lunch hours vary from place to place, and alcohol is not included. Inquire when you make your reservations.

Downtown Disney

This enclave of shopping, dining, and entertainment has three distinct neighborhoods: the Marketplace, Pleasure Island, and the West Side. Within them, you'll find eateries such as Wolfgang Puck Café, House of Blues, Ghirardelli Ice Cream & Chocolate Shop, Planet Hollywood, Rainforest Cafe, and T-Rex: A Prehistoric Family Adventure. Overall, Downtown Disney provides a variety of fast food, table service, cheap eats, and super splurges. Downtown Disney is on Walt Disney World property and can be reached by car, resort bus, or (from select WDW resorts) ferry. Note that all branches of Downtown Disney's entertaining triumvirate are gate- and admission-free.

69

Hot Tip

DisneyQuest devotees note: The venue's resident Cheesecake Factory Express is no more. However, you can still tame that appetite you built up after hours of gaming without leaving the confines of DisneyQuest. An eatery called FoodQuest has taken over the space formerly occupied by C.F.E. Admission must be paid to enter DisneyQuest, and, therefore, to eat at the quick-service restaurant. It serves lunch, dinner, and snacks—and participates in the Disney Dining Plan.

Bongos Cuban Cafe (West Side)

L D S | **$$–$$$**

Spicing up the Downtown Disney dining repertoire with a menu driven by Cuban and Latin American flavors, this eatery was created, in part, by singer Gloria Estefan. Its slate of traditional and nouvelle Cuban dishes includes black bean soup (our preferred dish), plantains, steak topped with onions, and flan. The atmosphere here is quite lovely (and often lively). Indoors, the mosaic mural and palm-leaf railings set the scene; the patio for outdoor seating wraps around a three-story pineapple, easily our favorite part of this creatively designed restaurant. A take-out window provides snacks on the go. Diners are sometimes treated to live music (feel free to sway in your seat). A small shop sells items such as shirts and hats emblazoned with the Bongos logo. Reservations are available by calling 407-828-0999.

Cap'n Jack's Restaurant (Marketplace)

L D S $$–$$$ ❤

The Cap'n is a true Disney World legend, having the distinction of 30-plus years of seafaring service under his cap. His fare, like his look, remains timeless. The nautically themed pier house juts right out over Village Lake, providing water views from most vantage points. The appetizer menu is such—shrimp, clam chowder, and the like—that it's as good for lunch or dinner as it is for a snack. Entrées extend to jumbo lump crab cakes, salmon, pot roast, pasta dishes, and seafood specialties. There is a tempting variety of wines, beer, and other cocktails—and the house's signature frozen strawberry margaritas are classic.

Cap'n Jack's is a nice place to enjoy the late afternoon, as the setting sun streams through the picture windows. Reservations are recommended.

Earl of Sandwich (Marketplace)

B L D S $–$$ ❤

This tip-top counter-service establishment is brimming with sweet and savory possibilities. Among the fare standing by is a variety of hot and cold sandwiches (freshly prepared on warm bread), wraps, tossed salads, and homemade desserts. More exotic selections, such as Hawaiian BBQ (Hawaiian BBQ ham with fresh pineapple and Swiss cheese), The Original 1762 (warm roast beef sandwich with creamy horseradish sauce and cheddar cheese), and Caribbean Jerk Chicken are also served. The Veggie sandwich is also an option.

DOWNTOWN DISNEY

Breakfast items include sandwiches and baked goods. There are quite a few "grab and go" selections as well. Dessert can be cupcakes, fresh-baked cookies, muffin crowns, or English trifle. Beer, wine, and Kona coffee are on the menu, too. Ample seating is available inside the restaurant and at outdoor tables.

Fulton's Crab House (Pleasure Island)

L D S **$$$–$$$$**

This regal restaurant, originally known as the *Empress Lilly* (after Walt Disney's wife, Lillian Disney), occupies a three-deck riverboat. Though it looks as if it might set sail at any moment, the replica ship is permanently docked at the edge of Village Lake (near Portobello). Guests board the ship via gang-plank and are enveloped by polished woods, brass detailing, and nautical nostalgia.

The extensive (albeit pricey) dinner menu changes with the day's arrivals. It's not unusual for Alaskan wild halibut to be seen next to Panama City (Florida) snapper. Signature seafood dishes include Dungeness crab legs; a San Francisco-style seafood stew with king crab, shrimp, scallops, mussels and fish in a tomato broth; and crab and lobster platters. For landlubbers, bone-in rib-eye, filet mignon, and free-range chicken are satisfying choices.

For a quicker fix, visit our top choice here: the ravishing raw bar at the adjoining Stone Crab lounge. In fact, for a relatively reasonably priced lunch, it's lounge or bust. If the weather's pleasant, try for a table outside, on the bow of the ship. Reservations are recommended for the restaurant.

Ghirardelli Ice Cream & Chocolate Shop (Marketplace)

`S` `$-$$`

What is it about an old-fashioned ice cream parlor that makes just about everybody giddy? Oh, yes, the ice cream. This spot does it one better and throws in its famous chocolate, to boot. Stop in for a chocolatey treat, root beer float, or refreshing malt. If you've got a sweet tooth, this place delivers. Tables are available on a first-come, first-served basis. There is a walk-up counter, too. We often duck in here for a quick cup of coffee and a chocolate chaser. And there's always the potential for a free sample.

House of Blues (West Side)

`L D S` `$$-$$$`

With a distinctive southern-inspired menu (étouffée, jambalaya, barbecue, catfish nuggets, and the like) and rustic, folk art-studded design, this Disney-based member of the House of Blues family of restaurants doesn't disappoint. At the far west of the West Side, it's a satisfying spot for an afternoon meal, dinner, or a late-night bite. The enclosed Voodoo Garden is particularly inviting. Live music is presented in the restaurant and on the front porch on select days. There is a lively gospel brunch every Sunday. Reservations are recommended. To book a table, call 407-934-BLUE (934-2583).

Planet Hollywood (West Side)

L D S **$$–$$$**

Chances are, you'll have no trouble finding this restaurant—just keep your eyes peeled for the giant globe. Built on three levels, this colossal sphere is jam-packed with classic movie and television memorabilia.

The menu features salads, sandwiches, pasta dishes, burgers, appetizers, fajitas, and dessert specialties. Consider sampling the chicken crunch appetizer, Asian chicken salad, shrimp and bacon club sandwich, or lasagna. Bananas Foster is among the dessert choices. Reservations are recommended.

Portobello (Pleasure Island)

L D **$$$**

The "yacht club" decor has disappeared, and this longtime WDW favorite has been transformed into an Italian trattoria, with warm colors that match the rustic Italian cuisine. The best seats are on the waterfront porch, and even with a new menu, the wood-burning-oven pizzas are still a top choice. Traditional Italian cuisine includes mix-and-match antipasti, hand-crafted sausage, pastas, and fish.

At lunchtime, the menu includes Portobello's signature sandwiches, like the pesto-marinated chicken with fontina cheese. For dinner, try the ravioli gigante (filled with ricotta and spinach) with tomato, basil, and toasted garlic. The full-service bar offers a solid wine list of Italian favorites, specialty cocktails, and beer. For dessert, it's tough to resist the tiramisu.

Raglan Road Irish Pub (Pleasure Island)
L D S **$$-$$$**

A wee bit of the Emerald Isle can be found at Disney's Pleasure Isle. The convivial spot features furnishings crafted in Ireland, live music, and a menu with cuisine courtesy of Chef Kevin Dundon, one of Ireland's best-known culinary wizards. Think traditional Irish fare with a modern flair. Instead of plain old fish with your chips, expect lightly sautéed lemon sole. There is no admission charge to enter—be it for food or drink.

Rainforest Cafe (Marketplace)
L D S **$$-$$$**

Lush (and loud) as a jungle, this place is thick with tropical vegetation and fish-filled aquariums (not to mention the occasional thunderstorm). A talking tree offers a stream of ecological insights, and animal experts are on hand to field questions. Dishes have names like Mogambo (pasta with shrimp), Plant Sandwich (veggies), and Mojo Bones (barbecued ribs). Appetizers and desserts can be shared. Reservations can be made by calling the restaurant: 407-827-8500. Without them, expect quite a wait. Note that there is another Rainforest Cafe at Disney's Animal Kingdom. The Animal Kingdom location accepts reservations through 407-WDW-DINE (939-3463).

DOWNTOWN DISNEY

T-Rex: A Prehistoric Family Adventure (Marketplace)

L D $$–$$$

Dinosaurs throw one heck of a dinner party. See for yourself at this eye-popping new dino-themed, interactive feasting facility. When you enter, you'll be greeted by hosts we were all led to believe were extinct. Okay, they're life-size *mechanical* dinosaurs, but they're still pretty cool. As are the waterfalls, bubbling geysers, and fossil dig site. It's all so distracting, you may forget why you came here in the first place. When your stomach starts growling, plan to appease it with anything from Jurassic Salad to Prehistoric Pot Pie. With soup, sandwiches, pasta, seafood, and steaks, this place aims to please everyone. You'll find it near Fulton's Crab House at Downtown Disney Marketplace.

Wetzel's Pretzels (Marketplace and West Side)

S $

Salted or unsalted, buttery or plain—Wetzel's can satisfy most pretzel cravings. Among the choices are the Jalapeño Cheese Melt, the Sinful Cinnamon, and the Three-Cheese varieties. They sell ice cream, too.

Wolfgang Puck Café (West Side)

L D S $$$ 💙

One of four Walt Disney World establishments that bear the name Wolfgang Puck, this one offers some of the chef's best-known specialties. Among the spotlighted dishes are gourmet pizzas, Thai chicken satay, pasta with fresh vegetables, Chinois chicken salad, and rotisserie chicken. The menu is equal parts sophisticated and straightforward—and very fresh. Plan ahead and save room for dessert. The place is a bit noisy, but worth shouting over.

Sushi lovers take note: Housed within this space is a sushi bar that's as aesthetically appealing as it is palate-pleasing. You can order sushi at the bar and in the cafe. Reservations are recommended for the cafe.

🍽️ Wolfgang Puck Café— The Dining Room (West Side)
D $$$-$$$$

Don't be confused by the name. The Dining Room refers to a separate restaurant that just happens to be in the same building as Wolfgang Puck Café and Express. (We think of it as "Puck's Deluxe.") The formal upstairs Dining Room is devoted to the more elaborate of Wolfgang Puck's cuisine—for example, Chinois rack of lamb with a spicy cilantro-mint sauce and wasabi-infused potatoes. Reservations are recommended.

🏃 Wolfgang Puck Express (Marketplace and West Side)
L D S $-$$ 🐭

Wolfgang Puck turns his talents to fast service and signature treats. Among them are (delectable) wood-fired pizzas, rotisserie chicken, soups, sandwiches, grown-up-friendly mac and cheese, and salads—including his famous Chinois chicken salad. (The West Side location is tucked inside the Wolfgang Puck Café building, while the Marketplace spot is near the Disney's Days of Christmas shop.)

ATTENTiON, COFFEE SNOBS

Face it. For many of us, the magic doesn't start until that first sip of coffee makes its way past our lips. And not just any coffee will do. It must be a half-caf soy-milk latte with extra foam! In other words, we have great expectations. The bad news? The standard cup here is Nescafé. If you're a fan, you're in luck. If not, you may have to venture a bit to get a satisfying java jolt. The good news is, specialty coffee and espresso bars are easing their way onto the Disney scene. There's at least one in each theme park and some at the resorts. Select restaurants serve special coffee blends, too. Among our favorite spots:

- American Adventure (Epcot's World Showcase, a stand near the pavilion)
- Artist Point (Wilderness Lodge)
- Big River Grille & Brewing Works (BoardWalk resort)
- California Grill (Contemporary resort)
- Contemporary resort (lobby stand)
- Jiko—The Cooking Place (Animal Kingdom Lodge)
- Flying Fish Cafe (BoardWalk resort)
- Garden Grove (Swan resort)
- 40 Thirst Street (Downtown Disney Marketplace and West Side)
- Fresh—Mediterranean Market (Dolphin resort)
- Kona Cafe (Polynesian resort)
- Picabu (Dolphin resort)
- Starring Rolls Cafe (Disney's Hollywood Studios)

WDW RESORTS

Each of the nearly 30 resorts at Walt Disney World offers its own set of specially themed eateries. There are clambakes at the Beach Club, luaus at the Polynesian, wild game at the Wilderness Lodge, and beignets at Port Orleans French Quarter. Meals may be served buffet, family, or traditional table-service or fast-food style. Disney characters are often on hand (especially for breakfast), and some snack spots stay open 'round the clock. In fact, the resort dining scene has expanded and been upgraded so much of late that the (occasionally arduous) task of resort-hopping is a more worthwhile experience than ever before.

ALL-STAR RESORTS

🏃 Food Courts
B L D S **$–$$** 🎵

Each of the All-Star resorts features a
themed central food court. **All-Star Sports**
has **End-Zone** food court in **Stadium Hall**.
At **All-Star Music**, it's **Intermission** food
court in **Melody Hall**. And at the **All-Star
Movies** resort, it is the **World Premiere**
food court in **Cinema Hall**. The food courts
offer similar food stands—although Movies
is a cut above. (It's a bit bigger, brighter,
and more modern.) The selections include
pasta, pizza, burgers, hot dogs, sandwiches,
salads, snacks, and a wide variety of breakfast and baked goods, plus a selection of
"grab and go" items. Expect to find lots of
kid-pleasers.

ANIMAL KINGDOM
LODGE

🍽 Boma—Flavors of Africa
B D **$$–$$$** 🎵

Designed to resemble an African marketplace, Boma offers an impressively diverse
selection—the fare served represents 50
African countries. Though the eatery may be
described as "cafeteria style," this is not a
negative. It's one big buffet with multiple
stations, and the food is every bit as good as
what you'd expect in a fine dining place.

The all-you-can-eat affair provides an
excellent bang for your Disney dining buck.
Menu selections include wood-roasted meats

and grilled seafood, plus soups and stews (chicken corn porridge and smoked tomato among them) and a decidedly different watermelon rind salad; be sure to leave room for the decadent pastry known as the Amarula Zebra Dome. It's tempting to overeat at a bounteous feast such as this, so consider taking tiny portions of everything. You can go back for seconds of your favorites. The wine list includes selections from various African vineyards. Even if you're not staying at the Lodge, it's worth the trip. Reservations are recommended.

Jiko—The Cooking Place
D $$$–$$$$

Here at one of the most unusual Walt Disney World dining experiences, chef John Clark's cuisine is inspired by the tastes of Africa, with influences from around the globe. Start with one of the paper-thin flatbreads, like kalamata olive with five cheeses, or the cucumber, tomato, and red-onion salad with a watermelon vinaigrette. Chermoula chicken is a signature dish, and you'll always find the oak-grilled filet mignon with macaroni and cheese on the menu, too. End your meal with a fabulous cheese course, and/or sweets such as pistachio crème brûlée, or Tanzanian chocolate cheesecake.

The impressive wine list is exclusively South African, one of the most extensive collections in the U.S. This is an excellent choice for a grown-up splurge. Though it's hardly a kid favorite (the international, sometimes exotic cuisine may not appeal to timid palates), there are child-friendly menu options. Reservations are recommended. Incidentally, the word *jiko* is Swahili for "the cooking place."

 **The Mara**

B L D S **S–$$** ❤

This huge place near the pool has number of stations from which to order hot entrée selections. Guests walk up to the counter and place an order. After receiving their order, guests then pay at the cashier and grab a table. There's a substantial "grab and go" department, too. Among the pre-packaged options are sandwiches, salads, fruit, and bakery items.

 **Sanaa**

L D **$$–$$$** ❤

Pronounced *sah-NAH*, the name of this eatery means "artwork" in Swahili. The colorful dining room (in Kidani Village) has a family-friendly menu featuring Disney's take on African-Indian cuisine. Signature dishes include chicken or shrimp curry and beef short ribs slow-cooked in tandoor ovens. For lunch, we recommend the salad sampler. Even the burgers have an Indian touch, wrapped in soft, warm naan (a round flatbread). The breads with chutneys, pickles, and raita (yogurt dip) are lovely. Desserts introduce many tastes, from mango pudding to cardamom butter cake. Reservations are recommended.

BOARDWALK

Big River Grille & Brewing Works

L D S **$$–$$$** ❤

A standout for its fresh-brewed ales alone, this unassuming place delivers huge portions of pub grub. The straightforward-but-satisfying menu generally includes burgers and steaks. Sandwiches are a cut above. This restaurant tends to be more low-key than other BoardWalk eateries and makes for a peaceful retreat during the day. The interior has an industrial feel. We prefer to sit at outdoor tables on the boardwalk. Seating is available on a first-come, first-served basis.

🏃 BoardWalk Bakery

B L D S | **$** | 🐭

On any given morning, there are lines out the door of this tiny bakeshop next door to Kouzzina by Cat Cora. (If you're staying at the BoardWalk resort, this is one of the places to get your morning Nescafé.) The menu of fresh-baked goods includes muffins, dough-nuts, croissants, and cookies. They have sandwiches and salads, too.

🏃 ESPN Club

L D S | **$$–$$$** | 🐭

For sports fans, this joint is nothing short of a miracle. The spacious, welcoming, occasionally frenzied bar/family restaurant is a hard-core sports club. If there's a game being played, chances are it's on one of the million (okay, hundred—but it feels like a lot more) TVs. If not, a simple request may result in a channel change.

The fare includes burgers, wings that are larger and yummier than most, sandwiches, and a variety of salads and other entrées. Both the dining room and the bar area serve the full menu. Note that this establishment does not accept reservations. If you want to get a good seat, get there before game time. We love this place!

Flying Fish Cafe

D $$$-$$$$

Fun, sophisticated decor from the designer of the Contemporary's California Grill elevates the appeal—in fact, this restaurant could give most fine, big-city dining spots a run for their money. (Expect the tab to rival cosmopolitan hot spots, too.)

Chef Tim Keating is a wonderfully inventive chef, and his menu changes often. But you'll always find the signature potato-wrapped snapper with a creamy leek fondue and red wine and butter sauce, the crisp crab cakes, and a char-crusted New York strip steak. Though we've yet to be blown away by the service, the menu is worthy of the hefty price tag. Reservations are recommended. Diners *sans* reservations may ask to sit at the counter (when doing so, we prefer to sit as far from the open flames of the grill as possible—though we do enjoy the show).

NEW EATERY ALERT!

Kouzzina by Cat Cora has taken over the BoardWalk space formerly occupied by our old friend Spoodles. Featuring Mediterranean-style (with a Greek emphasis) cuisine, this tempting new dining venue is a participant in the Disney Dining Plan. For details or to make reservations, call 407-939-3463.

 Seashore Sweets

`S` `$`

A cheery, old-fashioned sweetshop, this spot sells homemade candies, saltwater taffy, heavenly homemade ice cream, sorbet, and frozen yogurt. It's next door to the Flying Fish Cafe.

CARIBBEAN BEACH

Old Port Royale Food Court

`B L D S` `$–$$` 🐭

A cluster of side-by-side, walk-up windows, this food court caters to families. **Market Street Grab and Go** serves croissants, freshly baked rolls, pastries, and other fresh-baked treats. Soups, salads, and hot and cold sandwiches make up the selections at **Montego's Deli**. Burgers and chicken sandwiches are among the offerings at **Port Royale Hamburger Shop**. In addition to pizza, the **Royale Pizza & Pasta Shop** serves Italian specialties. **Bridgetown Broiler Shop** serves made-to-order omelets for breakfast and a selection of dinner items, such as carved turkey and pork loin. There is a spacious dining area, so it's usually easy to get a table. There is outdoor seating, too.

Shutters at Old Port Royale

`D S` `$$–$$$` 🐭

The dining room here is as kid-friendly as a table-service eatery can be. Some menu highlights include New York strip steak, Caribbean pasta, and pork ribs. The restaurant

WDW RESORTS

is in the resort's Old Port Royale building, across from the food court. In addition to soft drinks, beer, wine, and cocktails are served. Reservations are recommended.

CONTEMPORARY

 **California Grill**

D **$$$–$$$$** ❤

The West Coast theme shines through in such dishes as grilled pork tenderloin with balsamic vinegar-smothered mushrooms and polenta. The wine list is a mix of greatest hits and good finds. (At press time, several vintages were available by the glass.) Also drawing a crowd: the Grill's flatbreads, sushi bar, and a host of vegetarian choices. The goat-cheese ravioli appetizer is a favorite.

Fresh desserts along the lines of warm Valrhona chocolate cake provide the finishing touches, and there are sweeping views of the Magic Kingdom (from select seats).

The small-but-spectacular sushi bar, set within the restaurant, is always crowded and never fails to elicit raves. The din in the dining room may impede quiet conversation. Servers occasionally seem to be spread too thin, but the food is first-rate. It can be chilly—bring a sweater. Reservations are necessary and must be booked with a credit card. Changes or cancellations must be made at least 24 hours ahead to avoid the $20 per person fee. This is a Disney Dining Plan "signature" restaurant.

An outdoor area (exclusively available to California Grill patrons) affords bird's-eye views of the Magic Kingdom. All guests must check in on the hotel's second floor and are directed to California Grill's express elevator.

 The Wave
B L D **$$–$$$** 🦫

Casual and fun, The Wave brings a surge of dining ideas to Disney. Starting at breakfast with organic Columbian coffee, make-your-own muesli (cereal) and a "Mega-Berry Smoothie," you know this is going to be different. At lunch, seasonal soups, oversized salads, and a vegetarian sandwich vie for attention with a classic reuben and bacon cheeseburger. At dinner, we highly recommend the sustainable fish of the day with edamame (soybean) stew or grilled flank steak with chimichurri. You can end on a sweet note with the mini-desserts (don't miss the panna cotta).

The wine program, with only screw-cap wines, focuses on bright-style New World wines from the Southern Hemisphere (an impressive 50 choices are available by the glass). Beer fans get certified organic ales from Orlando Brewing. Reservations are recommended. The cool adjacent lounge is perfect for an aperitif or after-dinner drink.

Chef Mickey's
B D **$$–$$$** 🦫

Sprawling across the cavernous fourth floor of the Contemporary is one of the biggest kid pleasers at Walt Disney World. Here, Chef Mickey and his friends host a buffet feast. The changing menu takes advantage of seasonal offerings; a sundae bar provides a sweet finish.

At some point during the meal, Chef Mickey will stop by your table, as will several of his friends. Be prepared to drop your fork and swing your napkin with Mickey on a moment's notice. Reservations are a must.

 **Contempo Café**

B L D S **$–$$** 🐭

If you head to the first floor in search of the snack bar that's been there since 1971, you're in for a surprise: it moved! All the way to the fourth floor. Peruse the menu on electronic boards with color photos, place your order, then head to the cashier. A pager blinks when food is ready for pick-up. Thin-crust pizzas, sandwiches, and soups of the day are among the selections. A "grab and go" section has drinks, salads, and fresh fruit. Note that this spot generally closes before midnight.

CORONADO SPRINGS

 **Maya Grill**

B D **$$$** 🐭

Guests here dine inside a Mayan pyramid, beside a volcano (dormant, of course). The menu features a bit of everything: seafood, meat, and poultry, with a touch of Latino spices added to some of the creations. The pulled-pork empanada and crabmeat chalupa are interesting starts to dinner, but you can always stick with a simple shrimp cocktail. Entrées range from St. Louis-style ribs and pan-seared duck breast to salmon filet, with many dishes cooked over an open-pit wood-fire grill. Reservations are recommended.

Pepper Market

B L D S **$–$$** 🐭

Modeled after an open-air market, there is a large seating area and lots of food stands to choose from. The place is a food court with a twist: Upon arrival, guests are escorted to a table by a host or hostess and presented with a napkin and a ticket. After that, it's self-service. Would-be diners step up to stands where vendors sell pizza, sandwiches, salads, burgers, stir-fry, Mexican specialties, baked goods, margaritas, and more. Items are logged on the aforementioned ticket. Just about anything can be ordered "to go." Everything is paid for at meal's end, as guests file past the cashier at the exit. Note that a ten percent gratuity is automatically included when you eat in the dining area. We aren't sure why.

DISNEY'S OLD KEY WEST

🏃 Good's Food to Go
B L D S **$** 🐭

A walk-up window with a simple menu: hamburgers, cheeseburgers, grilled chicken

IN-ROOM REFRIGERATORS

Hotel rooms in "deluxe" and "moderate" WDW resorts come with mini fridges. Guests staying at "value" resorts may rent a fridge for about $10 a night. Request it when you book the room, and confirm before arrival. They take up room, but the fridges are handy for milk and baby products, snacks, and small amounts of groceries. Guests who must refrigerate medical supplies will not be charged for refrigerator use (a copy of the prescription may be required).

DINNER AT SEA

For Disney's ultimate dinner-and-a-show splurge, consider reserving the elegant *Grand 1* yacht. You and up to 17 lucky invitees can enjoy a private tour of the lakes near the Magic Kingdom capped off with a viewing of Wishes, the park's fireworks show—all the while devouring delightful delicacies prepared by chefs at the Grand Floridian resort. The possibilities range from an intimate cruise for two, complete with dinner and champagne, to a swinging cocktail party for 18, with a boatload of shrimp, chips, wings, beer, and wine.

It costs about $450 (plus tax) per hour to rent the 5-room floating fantasyland. Driver and deckhand are included; refreshments are not. To book, call 407-824-7529 at least 24 hours and up to 180 days ahead. To cater the affair, call 407-824-2578. The *Grand 1* docks at the Grand Floridian but can pick up passengers at the Contemporary, Polynesian, and Wilderness Lodge.

sandwiches, salads, ice cream, and breakfast selections are among the offerings.

Olivia's Cafe
B L D **$$–$$$**

We thoroughly enjoy the Key West manner with which Olivia's approaches its theme. The laid-back setting and menu convey the spirit of the leisure-centric locale. Breakfast

WDW RESORTS

selections include eggs, pancakes, breakfast burritos, and more. Later in the day, look for items such as salads, conch chowder, onion rings, baked mahimahi, crab cakes, great cheeseburgers and specialty sandwiches, and apple pie, too. Wine, beer, and cocktails are served. The menu changes seasonally. Reservations are recommended.

FORT WILDERNESS

Trail's End Restaurant
B L D S **$–$$** ✿

True, it's a bit out of the way for anyone but Fort Wilderness guests (and even for some of them!), but for many, this rustic and unassuming spot is well worth the trip.

The informal log-walled restaurant offers a reasonably priced, all-you-can-eat breakfast (arguably one of the biggest bargains on Disney World property). The fare's not exactly gourmet, but it is bountiful. Buffet selections include grits, biscuits, gravy, and a tasty "breakfast pizza" that vaguely resembles an omelet. Lunch features chicken, pizza, soup, and chili. For dinner, expect smoked pork ribs, peel-and-eat shrimp, fried chicken, carved meats, a salad bar, and a variety of sides and dessert items. Pizza and other light items are available every night from 4 P.M. until 10 P.M. Beer, wine, and soft drinks are served. Reservations are recommended. Breakfast costs about $12 for adults, $8 for kids; lunch is about $13 for adults, $9 for kids; dinner is about $19 for adults, $11 for kids. After the meal, many guests chat and relax in the rocking chairs on the front porch.

GRAND FLORIDIAN

🍽 Cítricos
D | $$$–$$$$ | 🐭

From the aromas wafting from the open kitchen, it's clear that the chef has vowed to wow you with cuisine from the Americas and the Mediterranean herb by fragrant herb. The fare varies seasonally, but may include such items as sautéed shrimp with tomato, lemon, and feta cheese; or braised veal shank. Adventurous adult palates are most at home here. The menu's not extensive, but the wine list is. The menu suggests a wine to pair with an appetizer, entrée, and dessert. There is a private party room for parties of up to 12. Reservations are recommended.

🏃 Gasparilla Grill & Games
B L D S | $–$$ | 🐭

The mainstays at this 24-hour snack bar near the marina are grilled chicken, burgers, pizza, hot dogs, and soft-serve ice cream. Fruit, cereal, packaged snacks, soft drinks, beer, and wine are also available. There is indoor and outdoor seating. We prefer to eat outdoors beside the marina, as opposed to noshing next to the noisy arcade games. Items may be ordered "to go." Continental breakfast is also available.

🍽 Grand Floridian Cafe
B L D | $$$ | 🐭

A pleasant spot any time of day (there's so much old-world atmosphere here, you'd almost expect to see ladies twirling parasols in the midday sun and Scott Joplin playing

ONE LUMP OR TWO?

Teatime with all the à la carte trimmings—scones, tiny sandwiches, and pastries served on bone china—is at 2 P.M. in the Garden View Tea Room at the Grand Floridian. A large selection of teas (some custom blends are made exclusively for this establishment) and tasty accompaniments are offered every day until approximately 4:30 P.M. Reservations are recommended.

"The Entertainer" on a grand piano), the cafe is a relatively reasonably priced, low-key way to check out the poshest WDW resort.

The à la carte breakfast extends a bit beyond the usual fare. Lunch and dinner menus vary with the season but have traditional American dishes: onion soup, burgers, and the signature Grand Floridian sandwich. The wine selection is excellent. Reservations are recommended, but it may be possible to get a table if you're willing to wait. The restaurant is closed between 11 A.M. and 11:45 A.M.

 Narcoossee's
D $$$–$$$$ ❤

Named for a nearby Central Florida town, Narcoossee's specializes in fresh fish dishes —with the occasional land-based entrée making surf-and-turf combinations a decadent possibility. The menu has upscale selections (and prices), but the atmosphere is casual and, more than occasionally, clamorous. The display kitchen presents dishes such as steamed mussels, wild salmon, fresh Maine lobster, and filet mignon. The international wine selection is quite good—you might even enjoy a pre-dinner glass on the veranda. The view of the Seven Seas Lagoon and the Magic Kingdom (in the distance) completes the experience. Reservations are recommended.

1900 Park Fare
B D **$$$** 🐭

The atmosphere is reminiscent of an old-time amusement park, but the sophisticated buffet menu and subtle decor make this one of the most elegant character restaurants on the property. Mary Poppins and friends (characters vary) mingle with guests during the bountiful daily breakfast. Cinderella and her cronies visit the dining room during the dinner hours. Keep in mind that the lineup of characters does change from time to time.

Dinner features hot and cold seafood, pastas, vegetables, breads, and prime rib. The offerings change weekly, and some may be customized. A salad bar and dessert bar stand nearby. There's a special children's buffet, too. It offers hot dogs, burgers, pizza, chicken nuggets, and a fresh vegetable medley. The restaurant's focal point is Big Bertha, a band organ built in Paris nearly a century ago. She sits in a proscenium and rises 15 feet above the floor, occasionally bursting into a musical serenade, simultaneously playing pipes, drums, bells, cymbals, castanets, and a xylophone. Reservations are recommended.

Victoria & Albert's
D **$$$$**

This elegant dining room has the distinction of being Central Florida's only five-diamond restaurant, an honor awarded by AAA. It is indulgent without being too haute to handle (although the steep prices may curb your enthusiasm) and is considered by many to be the *grande dame* of the Disney dining scene.

The seven-course prix fixe menu changes often, always offering a selection of fish, poultry, and beef as main courses. But the beauty of this high-end experience is all the little tastes as you make your way through the $125-per-person adventure. You might start with lobster or quail, then move on to seared wild turbot or pork tenderloin. The cheese course is worth every calorie. And, even with seven courses, you must reserve room for the indulgent desserts: a flurry of soufflés, chocolate, and more. Perfect portions keep it all surprisingly manageable. The strains of a harp or violin provide a romantic backdrop. The wine list is encyclopedic. Wine-pairing is available for an additional $60 per person (let your server know about any personal wine preferences).

At the end of the meal, guests are given a souvenir menu and a red rose (ladies only). In sum, though the experience is an extremely expensive one, for many it is also quite special. Jackets are required for men. Guests must be at least 10 years old to dine here. Reservations are necessary.

POLYNESIAN

Capt. Cook's
B L D S **$–$$** ❤

The Captain dispenses snacks and light fare (both prepared and made to order) 24 hours a day. It's a good spot for breakfast items, burgers, flatbreads, Asian noodle bowls, salads, sushi, sandwiches, yogurt, fruit, and snacks. Milk (plain and chocolate), beer, wine, and soft drinks are also available. There's seating both indoors and out. Come here to buy and fill the Poly's refillable mug.

Kona Cafe
B L D S | **$$–$$$** | ❤

Warm colors, soft lighting, and South Seas decor render the crisp, fluid design of this dining space cozy and casual. The menu tends toward the exotic side as far as Disney restaurants are concerned, but there's a nice variety of items to select from. Lunch and dinner menus feature Asian-influenced entrées. Possibilities include teriyaki beef, slow-roasted prime rib, macadamia-crusted mahimahi, and char-crusted strip sirloin in a teriyaki marinade. The morning meal features a more traditional menu. Many java junkies claim that the coffee here is the best you'll find on Walt Disney World property. Reservations are recommended.

'Ohana
B D | **$$$** | ❤

'Ohana delivers a classic Disney experience. It's a meticulously themed, family-friendly restaurant, complete with entertainment. An interesting twist of note: 'Ohana's family-style dinner experience—a South Pacific feast prepared in the restaurant's open-fire cooking pit—does not come with a menu, so no decisions need to be made. The oak-grilled skewers of turkey, pork, and beef just keep coming. Potatoes au gratin with Maui onions, shrimp, and sesame coriander sticky wings are among the accompaniments, and coconut bread pudding served à la mode with Bananas Foster sauce is included for dessert. Soft

HOTEL PLAZA BLVD. RESORTS

The properties on Hotel Plaza Blvd.—
Best Western Lake Buena Vista,
Doubletree Guest Suites, Regal Sun,
Hilton, Royal Plaza, Buena Vista
Palace, and Holiday Inn at Walt Disney
World—sit inside WDW boundaries,
but are neither owned nor operated by
Disney. To make dinner reservations,
inquire at the hotel's front desk. Note
that Holiday Inn was being refurbished
at press time and will not be open in
early 2010. Here's the lowdown:

Best Western Lake Buena Vista

Trader's Island Grill serves breakfast
and dinner. The **Parakeet Café** offers
three meals, plus snacks and to-go
items. **Flamingo Cove** serves lunch
and cocktails. **Pizza Hut Express**
offers pizza (to eat in or take out).

Doubletree Guest Suites

A full-service restaurant and pool bar
offers a breakfast buffet, lunch, and
dinner, plus snacks, sandwiches, and
cocktails throughout the day. A market
has snacks and groceries.

Regal Sun

LakeView Restaurant serves breakfast, lunch, and dinner; Disney characters come for breakfast on Tuesday,
Thursday, and Saturday. **Sundial Cafe
24-7**, located in the lobby and open

Continued on page 99

drinks are included. Beer, wine, and cocktails cost extra.

'Ohana's setting, which features wood carvings under a vast thatched roof, is rather festive. So much so that there are periodic, boisterous hula hoop, limbo, and coconut-rolling contests for the little ones. Polynesian singers entertain from time to time.

Breakfast is also a family affair—make that extended family, as Lilo, Stitch, Mickey, and Pluto host a morning character meal. Breakfast fare is basic and presented family-style. (Platters are shared by the whole party.) Reservations are recommended.

POP CENTURY

🏃 Everything Pop!
B L D S $-$$ 🔴

The selection at this colorful, modern food court has included pasta, pizza, chicken, roast turkey, Asian dishes, burgers, hot dogs, sandwiches, salads, breakfast items, and baked goods (tie-dyed cheesecake!). Feel free to join the cast members as they dance the Twist at 8 A.M. and the Hustle at 6 P.M.

PORT ORLEANS FRENCH QUARTER

🏃 Sassagoula Floatworks & Food Factory
B L D S $-$$ 🔴

A food court with a Mardi Gras theme, this spot offers pizza, pasta, gumbo, burgers,

Continued from page 97

24 hours, supplies continental breakfast and light fare around the clock. For drinks, there's **Eclipse Bar** and **Horizons Bar**.

Buena Vista Palace Hotel & Spa

The lakeside **Watercress Cafe** serves breakfast and lunch only (Disney characters are in attendance Sunday mornings); the **Watercress Mini Market** is open from 6 A.M. to midnight for baked goods and sandwiches; **Outback Restaurant** (which, despite the name, is not part of the national chain) offers seafood and steak; the **Lobby Lounge** provides a place to sip a glass of fine wine; while armchair quarterbacks get a surge of adrenaline (and suds) at **Kook Sports Bar**.

Hilton

Adiamo Italian Bistro & Grille offers American and Italian fare, while **Benihana Steakhouse & Sushi** serves Japanese favorites. Both serve dinner only. **Covington Mill** serves breakfast (with Disney characters in attendance on Sunday) and lunch only. **Rum Largo Poolside Bar & Cafe** offers burgers, sandwiches, salads, and tropical drinks alfresco. **Main Street Market**, open 24 hours, is part deli, part country store.

Continued on page 100

Continued from page 99

For light meals, snacks, or drinks, drop by **John T's Lounge**; specialty coffees and ice cream are served at **Mugs**.

Holiday Inn at Walt Disney World
The newly remodeled hotel has several dining options. The **Atrium Restaurant & Lounge** offers three meals a day. **Pizza Hut** dispenses pizza. It has "grab and go" items, too.

Royal Plaza
The **Giraffe Café** offers breakfast and dinner. Kids ages 10 and under eat breakfast for free with a paying adult.

sandwiches, soups, salads, spit-roasted chicken, barbecued ribs, ice cream, and bakery products, including beignets.

PORT ORLEANS RIVERSIDE

Boatwright's Dining Hall
B D **$$–$$$** ❤

Southern specialties and American comfort food are the big draw here—think prime rib and jambalaya. For breakfast, we favor the banana-stuffed French toast. Beer, wine, and cocktails are available, as are soft drinks. The restaurant is quite popular, and, as the resort's only table-service eatery, it's tough to get in without a reservation. Be sure to book ahead.

WDW RESORTS

 Riverside Mill

B L D S | **$–$$** ✦

This food court disguised as a cotton mill (complete with working waterwheel) boasts half a dozen food counters and a sprawling seating area. Expect to find pizza, pasta, fried and grilled chicken, roast turkey, flank steak, burgers, salads, sandwiches, fresh baked goods, ice cream, and other snack selections. There's ample seating, so it's usually possible to get a table even during the busiest of times.

For guests on the go, the food court's deli does double duty as a convenience store, stocking sandwiches, juice, beer, wine, snack items, and salads.

SARATOGA SPRINGS RESORT & SPA

Artist's Palette

B L D S | **$–$$** ✦

Set in a converted artist's loft within Walt Disney World's sprawling resort, this spot offers breakfast, lunch, and dinner. Among the selections are fresh tossed salads, made-to-order sandwiches, pizza, baked goods, and more. There is an assortment of grocery items to choose from, as well as "grab and go" selections.

The Turf Club Bar & Grill

L D S | **$$** ✦

A restaurant-within-a-lounge with an old-fashioned horse-racing theme (and a pool table), this eatery serves burgers,

sandwiches, salmon, chicken, snacks, and more. There is a big-screen TV, too. Reservations are recommended.

SWAN & DOLPHIN

Cabana Bar & Grill
L S **S**

Burgers, grilled chicken sandwiches, fruit, and yogurt are offered at this poolside eatery. There is a full bar. It is located near the Dolphin.

The Fountain
L D S **$$**

Themed as a sophisticated soda fountain, the Dolphin Fountain is a sleek, inviting place to stop for a meal or a sweet snack. Homemade ice cream is the obvious highlight here. Flavors have included dark chocolate, cappuccino, and mint chocolate chip. Burgers, sandwiches, and salads may also be available.

Fresh—Mediterranean Market
B L **$$–$$$**

If you need a quick bite but are looking for more than fast food, Fresh may fit the bill. The menu is simple, but it offers a little something for everyone. Expect the menu to include salads, sandwiches, soups, and simple entrées with fish, chicken, and pasta. No surprises, just satisfying fare. They serve fresh-brewed Starbucks coffee, too. You'll find this eatery on the Dolphin resort's first floor, next to The Fountain.

MEALS WiTH CHARACTER(S)

Character meals are the icing on the cake—or, in some cases, the whole cake—for many visitors to Walt's World. As with everything else here, dining with Donald, munching with Mickey, or chatting with Cinderella is the stuff of everlasting memories. Not surprisingly, these events are insanely popular, so be sure to get reservations (see page 10) to avoid disappointment. One other thing to note: the characters scheduled to appear can change at a moment's notice, and if you are expecting Mickey, you may get Minnie or one of their friends. Here's a rundown of the spots that invite you to dine with Disney characters (again, characters and other details may be different when you visit):

Akershus Royal Banquet Hall:
Belle, Jasmine, Snow White, Sleeping
  Beauty, Mulan, and Ariel (see page 38)

Cape May Cafe:
Goofy, Minnie Mouse, and Donald
  Duck (see page 111)

Chef Mickey's:
Mickey, Minnie, Chip, and Dale
  (see page 87)

Cinderella's Royal Table:
Cinderella and friends (see page 21).
  (Cinderella greets guests in the lobby,
  while princesses host breakfast and
  lunch. Fairy Godmother's here all day.)

Continued on page 104

Continued from page 103

Crystal Palace:
Winnie the Pooh, Tigger, Eeyore, and Piglet (see page 26)

Garden Grill:
Chip and Dale (see page 35). Mickey and Pluto may join the fun.

Garden Grove:
Goofy and Pluto host breakfast at the Swan resort (see page 105). Timon and Rafiki join them for dinner.

Hollywood & Vine:
Enjoy breakfast and lunch with Playhouse Disney characters Jo Jo and Goliath and *Little Einsteins'* June and Leo (see page 58).

Mickey's Backyard Barbecue:
Mickey Mouse and friends entertain at this Fort Wilderness dinner show (see page 114).

1900 Park Fare:
Stars like Mary Poppins appear at breakfast. Cinderella and friends (see page 94) are here for dinner. Alice and the Mad Hatter host the Wonderland Tea Party.

'Ohana:
Mickey, Lilo, Stitch, and Pluto (see page 96)

Tusker House:
Donald Duck and friends (see page 67)

Garden Grove
BLDS **$$–$$$**

This Swan eatery means to transport guests
to the peaceful gardens of New York's
Central Park—and the 25-foot oak tree is a
most realistic touch. The restaurant offers a
full breakfast menu, and salads, sandwiches,
and creatively prepared entrées for lunch.
What's the dinner "special"? It comes with
a side of Disney characters! Different nights
also bring different fare. At press time,
Wednesday and Saturday were featuring
barbecue; Sunday, Tuesday, and Thursday
offered Italian selections; and Monday and
Friday served up seafood. In addition to all
dinners, Disney characters are on hand
for breakfast on Saturday and Sunday.
Reservations are recommended. Pay a visit
to *www.swandolphin.com* for details.

Il Mulino New York Trattoria
D **$$$–$$$$**

A swank Swan destination, Il Mulino offers
upscale Italian cuisine in a relaxed yet
vibrant bistro-like setting. Specializing in
piatti per il tavolo, or family-style dining,
the spot is ideal for groups. The seasonal
menu is characterized by blends of seasonal
ingredients drawn from the Abruzzi region
of Italy. Signature items include *gamberi al
mulino* (jumbo shrimp with spicy cocktail
sauce), *gnocchi bolognese* (potato dumplings
with meat sauce), *pollo fra diavolo* (chicken
in a spicy red sauce), and *salmone* (sautéed
salmon in garlic and olive oil with wild
mushrooms and broccoli rabe). *Mangia!*

All dinners begin with an antipasti tasting,
on the house. Enjoy it while perusing the wine
list's 250 or so Italian varietals. The children's

WDW RESORTS

menu includes pepperoni pizza, fettuccine alfredo, and chicken parmigiana. To make a reservation, call 407-939-3463 or 407-934-1199; or visit *www.swandolphin.com*.

Kimonos

D S **$$–$$$**

In the mood for sushi with a side of karaoke? You've come to the right place! This Swan lounge is an honest-to-goodness karaoke bar (the only one at WDW). Some guests come to sing, while others are drawn by the sushi. This spot opens around dinner time, serving food and drinks. The singing generally gets started at about 9 P.M. or so. A good time is generally had by all.

Picabu

B L D S **$$**

A combination cafeteria and convenience store, this Dolphin destination serves sandwiches, salads, burgers, pizza, and more. The adjoining convenience store offers snacks and sundries. It's a tad pricey as fast food goes, but the fare's a cut above average, too. The house coffee is Starbucks. This eatery (and the convenience store inside it) stays open 24-7. Prices tend to run higher than your average WDW snack bar.

Shula's

D **$$$$**

Like the original Shula's in Miami, this Dolphin dining spot specializes in generous portions of certified Angus beef, in addition to chicken and fresh fish dishes. The upscale eatery pays tribute to the 1972 Miami Dolphins—that was the year coach Don Shula led his team to a perfect NFL season. Photos abound, and the menu comes

RESORT TO RESORT

If you're staying in one resort and dining in another, you need to plan ahead—even if the resorts are linked by monorail or water taxi. Why? The transportation may be operating before dinner, but if you're out late enough you'll have to get yourself home another way.

The good news is you will never be stranded. Bus transportation runs until about 2 A.M.—but it's not direct. If the theme parks are closed, you'll have to take a bus to Downtown Disney and transfer to a bus to your hotel. If the theme parks are open, you can take a bus to any park and transfer to one that's headed to your resort. Keep in mind that the trip can take up to 90 minutes in either direction. If that thought is unpleasant, do what we sometimes do: splurge on a cab. Taxis should run between about $7 and $22, depending on the destination. If you have more than three people in the party, request a van. Ask at your resort's bell services desk.

on an autographed football. The prices are a bit steep, but the steaks are definitely top-notch and lovingly prepared. Though the interior celebrates the game of football, this is not a casual sports bar. The dress code is business or resort casual. Reservations are recommended. Don't ask for a kids' menu—they don't have one. FYI: This restaurant is a seven-time winner of *Wine Spectator*'s Award of Excellence.

Splash Terrace

L S **$**

A poolside snack bar, this stand serves burgers and other grilled fare, as well as ice cream. Soft drinks, beer, wine, and frozen specialty cocktails are available, too. An assortment of packaged snacks is also on hand.

Todd English's bluezoo

D **$$$–$$$$**

A sophisticated member of the Disney dining scene, the menu at this Dolphin spot features coastal cuisine, incorporating an innovative selection of fresh seafood with both international and New American culinary influences. The raw bar's stocked with juicy (if a tad pricey) oysters and littleneck clams. If you prefer your seafood cooked, try the chilled poached jumbo shrimp or chilled Maine lobster tail. A popular starter is the brothy clam chowder with salt-cured bacon and oyster crackers. All of the entrées are tempting: from miso-glazed Chilean sea bass to bacon-wrapped tuna to bluezoo's dancing fish (roasted on a rotating spit).

Not in the mood for a selection from the sea? Consider braised pork, flame-grilled beef tenderloin, or the chef's pasta of the day. If you've got room when the dessert menu arrives, expect to be tempted by sweets such as warm chocolate cake and banana cream tart with roasted pineapple. Reservations are recommended. Note that it's possible to get food service at the bar (all menu items are available), a plus for small groups or solo diners. Closing time at the bar tends to vary (depending on just how crowded the place is). It's better to get here on the early side.

WILDERNESS LODGE

 Artist Point
D **$$$–$$$$** ♥

The Pacific Northwest theme of this top-notch if under-appreciated restaurant is announced in landscape murals, while tall red-framed windows look out to Bay Lake. The cavernous dining room is by no means intimate, but it's not without charm.

Artist Point's hallmark is its knack for translating fresh, seasonal ingredients from the Pacific Northwest into flavorful creations. An excellent example is the freshly flown-in salmon served on a smoking cedar plank. The menu may include beef, veal, buffalo, venison, and chicken selections. The wine list features many vintages, including some of the best pinot noirs and syrahs from Oregon and Washington State.

The desserts are worth making room for, no matter how full you think you are; it's just the fork-licking finale you'd expect from a restaurant of this caliber. Many guests swear by the berry cobbler, which is far from the traditional. Ask your server for a description. The cumulative effect here is an artist's palette for the sophisticated palate. Reservations are recommended.

Roaring Fork
B L D S **$** ♥

Set in a stone-walled area (a bit dungeon-like, but in an appealing way), this elaborate snack bar serves salads, burgers, fries, sandwiches, chili, and snacks. Traditional breakfast items are available, as is a custom yogurt bar. Soft drinks, beer, and wine are also offered.

WDW RESORTS

📭 Whispering Canyon Cafe
B L D **$$$** 🐭

The name is ironic, as there is nothing quiet about this place. A family favorite, Whispering Canyon is one of the most boisterous Disney restaurants. All meals are offered à la carte and "all-you-can-eat" style. The latter means heaping plates keep coming to the table until you say "when."

Starting at the crack of dawn, the air is filled with aromas of bacon, sausage, and scrambled eggs. Lunch introduces pulled-pork sandwiches, salads, and desserts. For supper, expect such items as roast chicken and smoked pork ribs. Reservations are recommended.

YACHT & BEACH CLUB

🏃 Beach Club Marketplace
B L D S **$-$$** 🐭

The beachy setting extends to this snack bar/convenience store. In addition to freshly prepared menu items (sandwiches and salads), there are packaged food and "grab and go" selections—small salads, cheese and fruit plates, peanut butter and jelly sandwiches, baked goods, gelato, and more. There is some seating. If you buy a refillable mug, this is the place to fill 'er up.

📭 Beaches & Cream Soda Shop
L D S **$** 🐭

This classic American soda fountain is situated poolside at the Beach Club resort. From late morning until late evening it serves up burgers, chili dogs, and chicken Caesar salads—not to mention ice-cream sundaes, floats, shakes, malts, and sodas.

Cape May Cafe
B D **$$–$$$**

Goofy and his pals greet hungry Beach Club visitors each morning at this whimsical, beach umbrella-studded dining area. The breakfast buffet includes all the usual standards, plus a few specialties of the house. Breakfast doesn't disappoint, but dinner is the big event here.

Dinner is presented as an all-you-can-eat New England-style clambake buffet, and it is one of the most popular meals and best overall values. The tempting lineup includes mussels, fish, clams, peel-and-eat shrimp, corn on the cob, ribs, red-skin potatoes, chowder, and salads. Don't forget to save room for dessert. Soft drinks are included. Cocktails are available at an extra charge. Reservations are a must.

WDW RESORTS

Captain's Grille
B L D **$$-$$$** 🐭

An airy space (formerly known as Yacht Club Galley) with a subtle nautical theme, this spot serves steaks and seafood for the whole family. Breakfast offerings include a buffet and a full menu; lunch and dinner are à la carte. Reservations are recommended.

Hurricane Hanna's Grille
L D S **$** 🐭

You can get burgers, salads, sandwiches, ice cream, and soft drinks at this poolside spot. There is a full bar.

Yachtsman Steakhouse
D **$$$-$$$$** 🐭

You know you're in for a serious steak experience the moment you walk through the door: There's an actual butcher shop, complete with aging meats in the foyer. Elevated expectations? Maybe. But the Yachtsman delivers an experience to rival those of the most revered New York steak houses.

The generous portions begin with massive rolls and may continue with an appetizer, such as seared diver scallops. Of course, there's no skimping on the excellent and expertly prepared aged-beef entrées (New York strip steak, filet mignon, and chateaubriand, etc.), so good luck finding room for crème brûlée. The menu also includes chicken and seafood. As is common for the steak house milieu, the decor takes a backseat to the food. That said, the dining area is pleasant, with some secluded nooks suited for special occasions. Reservations are recommended.

WDW DINNER SHOWS

At Disney World, the name of the game is entertainment, so why should dinner be any different? In addition to venues where entertainment comes as a complementary side dish (Biergarten in Epcot, Cosmic Ray's in the Magic Kingdom, Sci-Fi Dine-In Theater in Disney's Hollywood Studios, to name just a few), there are three honest-to-goodness dinner shows to choose from. Given their popularity and longevity (the Hoop-Dee-Doo's been packing houses for nearly four decades), there's plenty of reason to plan ahead and book "dinner as event."

113

Hoop-Dee-Doo Musical Revue (Fort Wilderness) 🐭

This family favorite opened in 1974, and it's been going like gangbusters ever since. Every show begins with the stagecoach arrival of a troupe of singers and dancers who proceed to race toward the stage at Fort Wilderness resort's Pioneer Hall. What follows is about 105 minutes of whoopin', hollerin', singing, dancing, and audience participation in a frontier celebration. This being a dinner show, the entertainment comes with unlimited country vittles: ribs, fried chicken (if anything is cold, we request a hot replacement), salad, vegetable, and strawberry shortcake. Soft drinks, wine, and beer are included.

The gags are groaners, but the audience eats 'em up. It's all in the course of an evening at the Hoop-Dee-Doo Musical Revue, presented nightly at 5 P.M., 7:15 P.M., and 9:30 P.M. Cost is about $51 per adult and $26 for children (ages 3 through 9) in Category 3 seating; about $55 for adults and $27 for kids in Category 2; and about $60 for adults and $31 for kids in Category 1. (Category 1 provides the best views of the show.) Prices include tax and gratuity. Reservations are necessary.

The show is presented at Pioneer Hall at Fort Wilderness year-round. Allow yourself plenty of time to get there. The dining room is chilly, especially in the summer. Bring a sweater to combat the air-conditioning.

Mickey's Backyard Barbecue (Fort Wilderness) 🐭

It's called a barbecue, but it feels like a country picnic/party, complete with a live band, games for kids, food, and Disney characters.

Presented at an open-air pavilion at Fort Wilderness, the festivities begin with music by a country band. Guests may need little coaxing to get out on the floor to kick up their heels (the dance lessons help), and Disney characters join in the fun.

Dinner consists of barbecue favorites: ribs and chicken, corn on the cob, and baked beans. Beer, wine, and soft drinks are included.

It goes without saying that kids love it, but many couples appreciate it as an entertaining and unique Disney night out (somehow, line dancing with Goofy has a universal appeal). For big groups, it's a full-out party. The show is presented seasonally. Call 407-939-3463 for a schedule and to purchase tickets. The cost is about $45 per adult and $27 for kids ages 3 to 9. Prices include tax and gratuity. Reservations are recommended.

Hot Tip

Though outdoors, the Spirit of Aloha and Mickey's Backyard BBQ are sheltered and presented rain or shine—but the former may be canceled if the temperature drops below 50 degrees.

Spirit of Aloha (Polynesian Resort) ♥

A decidedly Disney luau show, the Spirit of Aloha invites guests to participate in a "traditional" island musical celebration. Set in the beachfront backyard of a Hawaiian house (at the Polynesian resort), the experience combines traditional music with more contemporary ditties from the Disney film *Lilo and Stitch*. The show, complete with hula skirts, ukuleles, and fire-knife dancers, takes guests on a whirlwind journey from New Zealand to Samoa. It all stems from a (scripted and hokey) premise about a family member who's moved away and lost touch with her roots. A planned visit from said family member prompts a gathering meant to stir up happy memories of island life.

Presented in an open-air dining theater in Luau Cove, the all-you-can-eat feast is influenced by the flavors of Polynesia. Menu items include roasted chicken, stir-fried rice, and vegetables. The kids' menu features PB&J sandwiches, mac and cheese, chicken drumsticks, and hot dogs. Beer, wine, soft drinks, and dessert are included. Cost is about $51 per adult and $26 for children (ages 3 through 9) in Category 3 seating; $55 for adults and $27 for kids in Category 2; and $60 for adults and $31 for kids in Category 1. (Category 1 provides the best views of the show.) Prices include tax and gratuity and are subject to change. Reservations are necessary.

Plan to arrive about 30 minutes early, and allow extra time for transportation. The show may be canceled due to bad weather.

BOOKING DINNER SHOWS

Dinner shows may be booked up to 180 days ahead by calling 407-WDW-DINE (939-3463). Groups of eight or more should call 407-939-7707.

A credit card number is required for all dinner show reservations. Also, it's very important to remember that cancellations for dinner shows must be made at least 48 hours prior to showtime to avoid paying full price.

To make reservations for Walt Disney World restaurants, dial 407-WDW-DINE (939-3463). The dinner shows are quite popular, so reserve as soon as possible.

WDW Pubs and Lounges

What distinguishes Walt Disney World pubs and lounges from many bars in the real world? Well, in addition to over-the-top theming, you can almost always get a savory nibble to accompany that cocktail. Most WDW lounges serve food, be it from their own menu, or from that of a neighboring restaurant. Hours vary according to venue, but the hot spots at Downtown Disney are usually hopping into the wee hours of the morning.

Theme Parks

ANIMAL KINGDOM

Dawa Bar

A thatched roof provides shade, while the sounds of African music (occasionally live) fill the air. A full bar, including Safari Amber beer, is available. It is beside the Tusker House restaurant in Harambe.

Rainforest Cafe

The colorful Magic Mushroom bar serves, among other things, fruit blends and specialty drinks. Bar stools resemble animal legs (hooves and all). The watering hole is attached to Rainforest Cafe. Admission to the Animal Kingdom is not necessary to enter. It's possible to order from the restaurant's menu from here, too (see page 65).

EPCOT

Rose & Crown Pub ❥

This watering hole—a veritable symphony of polished woods, brass, and etched glass—adjoins the Rose & Crown Dining Room in the United Kingdom pavilion (see page 48). British, Scottish, and Irish beers are available, along with a score of specialty drinks and appetizing snacks imported from the other side of the Atlantic. On special occasions, there may be live (and lively) piano music.

Sommerfest ❦

Just outside the Biergarten restaurant in Germany (see page 39), there's a shaded spot where soft pretzels, bratwurst, frankfurters, Black Forest cake, and German beer and wine are available.

DISNEY'S HOLLYWOOD STUDIOS

Tune-In Lounge

A sitcom living-room setting, with comfy couches and chairs, characterizes this lounge next to the 50's Prime Time Cafe. Waiters play the roles of sitcom "dads," and old TV sets play scenes from beloved sitcoms (all of which feature food). A full bar is available. Appetizers and entrées may be ordered from the attached restaurant (see page 56).

NO PROOF NECESSARY

Soft drinks, fruit juices, and specialty drinks *sans* alcohol are available at all Walt Disney World bars and lounges. Just ask the bartender.

Resorts

ALL-STAR RESORTS

Pool Bars

There are small poolside oases in All-Star
Movies, All-Star Music, and All-Star Sports:
Silver Screen Spirits, Singing Spirits, and
Team Spirits, respectively. Each serves a
selection of beer, wine, traditional cocktails,
and specialty drinks.

ANIMAL KINGDOM LODGE

Capetown Lounge and Wine Bar

A small lounge area within Jiko—The
Cooking Place, this spot offers a selection of
African wines and other spirited beverages.
Guests may order from Jiko's menu (see
page 81).

Sanaa

Located in the resort's Kidani Village, this
lounge is adjacent to the restaurant (see page

DID YOU KNOW?

At Epcot's Rose & Crown Pub (located in
the United Kingdom pavilion at World
Showcase) a specially designed ale warmer
can heat your Guinness to 55 degrees—the
temperature favored by some authentic
British pubs.

82) of the same name. South African beers and wines are the specialties of the house.

Uzima Springs
A poolside bar, this small spot serves drinks and snacks during pool hours.

Victoria Falls
A pretty, mezzanine-level lounge overlooking Boma—Flavors of Africa (see page 80) and a small waterfall, this bar serves beer and wine with African influences, as well as cocktails, soft drinks, coffee, and tea.

BOARDWALK

Atlantic Dance
This dance hall showcases music (and videos) from the 1970s, '80s, '90s, and today. There's a full bar and a selection of specialty drinks.

Belle Vue Lounge 🐭
A full bar accompanies old-time tunes from antique radios in this cozy lounge. Board games are available for on-site use.

Big River Grille & Brewing Works 🐭
A working brewpub, this is where patrons may order appetizers at the bar and sample the brewmaster's flagship ales and specialty beers (see page 82).

ESPN Club 🐭
The ultimate sports bar provides live broadcasts along with a menu of ballpark favorites. Occasional trivia contests (with prizes) invite participation by patrons. It's a sports fan's dream come true (see page 83).

Jellyrolls
Dueling pianos and lively sing-alongs are

the draw at this unique club, serving beer and other drinks. There is usually a cover charge of about $7 to $10. The piano players encourage requests. Don't forget to make the tip jar happy. Jellyrolls appeals to all ages, but guests must be 21 to enter.

Leaping Horse Libations
The poolside bar offers all manner of cocktails—including frozen ones—plus sandwiches in a carnival setting.

CARIBBEAN BEACH

Banana Cabana
Refreshing beverages (cocktails and soft drinks) are served at this poolside bar.

CONTEMPORARY

California Grill Lounge
Prime 15th-story digs afford an eye-level view of the Magic Kingdom fireworks. A selection of California wines, as well as other drinks, plus items from the restaurant menu, are offered in this tiny space within the California Grill restaurant (see page 86). This lounge seems to shrink more each time we visit, but it's still worth a trip.

Outer Rim
This small lounge overlooking Bay Lake serves all manner of cocktails. It's located on the Grand Concourse level of the resort, across from Contempo Café (see page 88).

Sand Bar ❦
A full bar is offered poolside, weather permitting. The frozen piña coladas are certainly something to write home about. Fast food in

the form of burgers, sandwiches, and salads is available at the adjacent counter area.

The Wave Lounge

On the first floor of the resort, this hip, spacious bar boasts a wine list that is all screw cap (yes, that's a *good* thing)— a quaffable selection of wines from the Southern Hemisphere. About 50 are available by the glass; tasting flights are a great choice for those who wish to sample multiple wines (and not get snockered). Also on tap: organic beers, ports, sherries, and specialty drinks. It's possible to order from The Wave restaurant's outstanding menu (see page 87). Our humble opinion? The Wave is one of the very best Disney World lounges.

CORONADO SPRINGS

Rix Lounge

Located in the resort's main building, this eye- and palate-pleasing lounge serves specialty drinks, beer, wine, and tapas-style appetizers (chorizo flatbread, seafood, and more). Cappuccino is an option. Music may be provided by a deejay or live band. This venue gets a big thumbs-up.

Siestas 🐭

Swimmers can take time out for burgers, sandwiches, tacos, and cocktails at this spot near the pool in the Dig Site area.

FORT WILDERNESS

Crockett's Tavern 🐭

Cocktails, beer, and wine are served in a rustic setting. The tavern is inside the Trail's End Restaurant (in Pioneer Hall). Snack items may be ordered from Trail's End.

GRAND FLORIDIAN

WDW PUBS & LOUNGES

Garden View

A view of the pool and garden area makes this lounge a pleasant place to meet for a drink or dessert. Traditional afternoon tea is also served each day. Reservations are recommended for tea. Note that the tea experience isn't meant to be rushed. Allow time to sip slowly. And come hungry, as you'll be tempted with sandwiches and sweets.

Mizner's

Named after the eccentric architect who defined much of the flavor of southeastern Florida's Gold Coast, this handsome retreat is on the second floor of the main building. Ports, brandies, beer, wine, cocktails, and appetizers are featured. The atmosphere is a bit subdued in the early evening but can be raucous as the hours wear on.

Narcoossee's ❤

This lagoonside bar-within-a-restaurant (see page 93) offers international wines, as well as beer, coffee drinks, and cocktails. It's nice to enjoy a drink on the veranda overlooking the Seven Seas Lagoon.

Pool Bar

A good standby with beer, frozen drinks, and fast-food items.

DISNEY'S OLD KEY WEST

Gurgling Suitcase

This pocket-size lounge on the Turtle Krawl boardwalk serves Key West specialties, along with a variety of cocktails, plus beer and wine.

Turtle Shack
Refreshments at this poolside spot include drinks and fast-food items.

POLYNESIAN

Barefoot Bar
An oasis next to the swimming pool, this bar serves beer, frozen drinks, and snacks. Item of note: frozen strawberry daiquiri. (We like it mixed with the piña colada.) It's possible to get alcohol-free concoctions, too.

Tambu Lounge
Adjoining 'Ohana restaurant, this small tiki bar offers appetizers, specialty drinks, and traditional cocktails in a tropical setting. There is a big-screen TV, but the view out the window is much more compelling. (Is that a volcano?) Note that this lounge serves as the waiting area for 'Ohana and can get quite busy during peak dining hours.

GOT i.D.?

The legal drinking age in the state of Florida is 21. However, just being 21 isn't enough to get served—you have to prove it. To do so, present a government-issued photo ID. If your driver's license doesn't have a photo, bring it *and* an official photo ID (a passport is ideal). Otherwise, you'll have to stick to soft drinks.

POP CENTURY

Petals

An assortment of specialty drinks, as well as beer, wine, and soft drinks are available at this colorful pool bar.

PORT ORLEANS FRENCH QUARTER

Mardi Grogs

Beer, specialty drinks, and a small selection of snack items are among the offerings at this poolside spot.

Scat Cat's Club

This New Orleans-style jazz lounge offers specialty drinks, appetizers, and occasional entertainment.

PORT ORLEANS RIVERSIDE

Muddy Rivers

The pool bar serves beer, several specialty concoctions, and fast-food items.

River Roost

Situated in a room designed as a cotton exchange, this lounge features specialty drinks, as well as light hors d'oeuvres.

SWAN & DOLPHIN

Cabana Bar & Grill

Beer, frozen drinks, and fast-food selections

are the main offerings at this Dolphin poolside spot.

Copa Banana
The tabletops in this Dolphin bar resemble oversize slices of fruit, and giant pineapples and palm trees offer a fitting backdrop for tempting tropical libations, as well as more traditional cocktails.

Kimonos
This Swan spot has a full bar and serves sushi and other treats. By night, it's a karaoke/sushi bar. Though big with the convention set, a good time is generally had by all. Come early to get a seat.

Lobby Lounge
The winding corridors of the Swan lobby have comfortable couches and chairs, punctuated by pianos where musicians often perform. A menu with international wines, ports, and cognacs is offered seasonally.

Shula's Lounge
This Dolphin watering hole in Shula's steak house features rich wood tones and comfy seating—the perfect place to sip a cocktail while playing armchair quarterback.

Splash Terrace
Beer, frozen drinks, and fast food are served at this Swan poolside cafe.

WILDERNESS LODGE

Territory Lounge
Located near Artist Point, this homage to explorers of the Old West is a nice spot for a pre-dinner treat. Appetizers, beer, wine, and specialty drinks are served.

Trout Pass

This poolside bar serves beer, wine, and frozen drinks.

YACHT & BEACH CLUB

Ale and Compass ✔

The tiny-but-charming lobby lounge proffers a full bar and has a nice specialty-drink menu (we think the Bloody Marys are rather special). They're known for their single-malt scotches, too. A light continental breakfast is served daily.

Crew's Cup

Styled after a traditional New England waterfront pub, this inviting lounge has a seafaring feel to it. It's next door to the Yachtsman Steakhouse, has more than 30 beers, and is a choice spot for a drink. There is an appealing appetizer menu, too.

Hurricane Hanna's Grille

This poolside spot, located near Stormalong Bay between the Yacht Club and Beach Club, offers specialty beverages, frozen drinks, and beer, as well as fast-food items.

Martha's Vineyard

While a full bar is available, wines from Martha's Vineyard (and other areas) are this spot's specialty. Appetizers are served.

Hot Tip

Wide World of Sports Cafe is open during select events at the Sports Complex. Call 407-WDW-DINE to see if it will be open during your visit. It is a Disney Dining Plan participant.

Downtown Disney

Bongos Cuban Cafe (West Side)

Housed inside a three-story pineapple is one of the more popular cocktail spots at Walt Disney World. There are booths and bar stools. It's possible to order food from the restaurant menu (see page 70).

Cap'n Jack's Restaurant (Marketplace) ❤

Agleam with copper and right on the water, this bar's specialty is its strawberry margaritas. The garlic oysters and clam chowder on the appetizer menu are great for a snack or a meal (see page 71).

Fuego (Pleasure Island)

Brought to you by Sosa Family Cigars, this small, chic spot features a bar that looks like a melting slab of ice. A full selection of libations are served, as are about 80 cigar brands and cigarettes. This is the only spot at WDW where guests may purchase tobacco products. And, yes, you can smoke here.

House of Blues (West Side)

While there is a traditional bar at the back of the restaurant, it's also possible to have drinks in the enclosed Voodoo Garden (table-service only). Guests may order from the restaurant menu (see page 73).

Raglan Road Irish Pub (Pleasure Island) ❤

Top o' the evenin' to you! This establishment simply oozes Irish charm. Stop in for a pint and a live music chaser. Guests may sit at tables (and order food) or by the bar. There is no admission charge. *Slainte!* (That's Gaelic for "cheers!")

Shark Bar (T-Rex: A Prehistoric Family Adventure; Marketplace)

Dive into this full-service bar (with an underwater theme) for specialty cocktails such as the T-Rita "cotton tinis." The bar itself resembles a big wave, and, in lieu of the usual tavern TV, patrons have a colorful aquarium to gaze upon while they imbibe or enjoy a selection from the restaurant's surprisingly sumptuous menu (see page 76). Though it's a family establishment (the place features a dinosaur theme, after all), Shark Bar is a grown-ups-only watering hole. You must show proper ID to belly up to the bar.

Stone Crab Lounge (Fulton's Crab House, Pleasure Island)

Head to the bow of the ship for one of the best scratch Bloody Marys around. They pair quite nicely with the establishment's oyster bar offerings (see page 72). A full selection of beverages (of both the spirited and virgin varieties) is served at a traditional bar and at tables. Reservations are not required, but guests who wish to snag a table should check in at the podium near the entrance.

Wolfgang Puck Café Bar (West Side)

Okay, it's technically a sushi bar (like that's a bad thing...), but this spot is also a great place to grab a stool and relax with an ice-cold beer. There is a TV (expect to see the local game of the moment) and a simple but savory menu— including selections of the aforementioned sushi (see page 76). It's a good choice when caught without a reservation.

WDW Recipes

Your Disney dining experience doesn't have to end when your vacation does. Though sweet souvenirs molded in the image of the Mouse may prove exceptionally satisfying, there may be more substantial culinary cravings to cure. Though your dining room isn't themed like a drive-in movie theater or a fairy-tale castle, and you rarely entertain princesses or 5-foot mice, it's still possible to whip up a little Disney magic in the privacy of your own kitchen. On the pages that follow, we've included seven of Walt Disney World's most requested recipes. Just add pixie dust.

New England Pot Roast

Savory pot roast is one of the most popular dishes in the Magic Kingdom's Liberty Tree Tavern (page 25), where an eighteenth-century ambience prevails and dinner is served family style.

¼ cup chopped garlic
¼ cup vegetable oil
3 pounds boneless beef shoulder
  roast
½ cup (1 stick) butter
1 cup all-purpose flour
1 cup Burgundy wine
6 cups beef broth
2 cups diced carrots
2 cups diced onions
2 cups celery, cut in large chunks
2 tablespoons chopped fresh thyme

1. Preheat oven to 350°F.

2. Sauté garlic in vegetable oil in a braising pan, then brown the meat. After meat is browned, remove from pan.

3. Melt the butter in the same pan, then stir in flour and continue cooking until flour is lightly browned.

4. Stir in Burgundy wine and beef broth.

5. Add carrots, onion, celery, and fresh thyme.

6. Place meat back in the pan. Cover and bake for 40 minutes to 1 hour, or until meat is tender.

Yield: 6 servings

Chef Mickey's Breakfast Pizza

This kid-pleasing dish is a great way to remember the good times at Chef Mickey's at Disney's Contemporary resort (page 87), where Mickey Mouse visits during breakfast and dinner.

One 12-inch precooked pizza shell
1 cup coarsely grated cheddar cheese
½ cup coarsely grated mozzarella cheese
½ cup coarsely grated provolone cheese
2 large eggs
¼ cup heavy cream
½ teaspoon salt, or to taste
Pinch of freshly ground black pepper, or to taste

1. Preheat oven to 375°F. Place pizza crust on a baking sheet.

2. In a medium bowl, blend the cheddar, mozzarella, and provolone cheeses.

3. In a small bowl, with a fork, beat together the eggs and the heavy cream, and season with the salt and pepper. Add to the cheese mixture.

4. Immediately, to avoid clumping, transfer the cheese mixture to the pizza shell.

5. Bake for 10 to 12 minutes, or until the cheese mixture is set and is beginning to brown. Cut into slices; serve hot.

Yield: 6 servings

133

Tonga Toast

This decadent, deep-fried breakfast favorite has been served for more than a quarter of a century at Disney's Polynesian resort, and is now on the menu at Kona Cafe (page 96).

1 cup sugar
2 teaspoons cinnamon
1 loaf sourdough bread (8 inches long)
2 bananas, peeled
1 quart canola oil, for frying

1. Mix the sugar and cinnamon with a fork until thoroughly blended; set aside.

2. Slice the bread into four 2-inch-thick slices.

3. Cut each banana in half crosswise, then cut each piece lengthwise.

4. Place a bread slice flat on the counter and tear out just enough from the middle (do not tear all the way through) to stuff half a banana into it; repeat with each slice of bread.

5. In a large pot or a deep fryer, heat the oil to 350°F; use a candy thermometer to make certain the oil does not get any hotter, or it will burn.

6. Gently place one bread slice into the oil for 1 minute, or until lightly browned.

7. Turn and fry for another minute on the other side.

8. Remove bread from the deep fryer and toss it in the sugar and cinnamon mixture. Repeat for each piece.

Yield: 4 servings

New England Clam Chowder

On a visit to Cape May, New Jersey, the chef collected this original recipe for "white" clam chowder served at Cape May Cafe at Disney's Beach Club resort (page 111). The creamy soup is a popular starter at the restaurant's nightly New England clambake.

½ cup (1 stick) butter
⅓ cup all-purpose flour
2 tablespoons vegetable oil
1 large onion, finely chopped
3 stalks celery, finely chopped
2 cups clam broth
3 medium-sized red potatoes, diced into
    ½-inch pieces (about 3 cups)
2 cans (6½ ounces each) chopped
    clams, liquid reserved
1 teaspoon dried thyme leaves, crumbled
½ teaspoon dried basil leaves, crumbled
½ teaspoon salt, or to taste
¼ teaspoon freshly ground pepper, or
    to taste
4 drops Tabasco sauce, or to taste
2 cups half-and-half

1. Melt butter in a 2-quart saucepan over medium heat. Add flour and cook, stirring constantly, for 3 minutes. Remove the saucepan from the heat and set aside.

2. Heat oil in a 4- to 5-quart Dutch oven over medium heat until hot but not smoking. Add chopped onion and celery and cook, stirring, about 5 minutes, or until the onion is softened.

3. Stir in the clam broth, potatoes, chopped clams with their liquid, thyme, basil, salt, pepper, and Tabasco sauce. Bring the mixture to a simmer over medium heat and simmer for 5 minutes, or until the potatoes are cooked through.

4. Add the half-and-half and bring to a low boil over medium-high heat. Slowly add the flour mixture, whisking constantly, until well blended. Reduce the heat to low and simmer for 10 minutes, stirring occasionally.

Yield: Serves 8 as a first course or 4 as a main course (2 quarts)

Crab and Artichoke Cakes

Though it isn't always on the menu, this decadently rich appetizer gets raves at Victoria & Albert's, at Disney's Grand Floridian Resort & Spa (page 94).

   1 cup diced artichoke bottoms (canned or
      frozen)
   1 pound lump crabmeat
   ¾ cup panko bread crumbs
   1 teaspoon finely chopped red onion
   ½ teaspoon chopped fresh herbs
      (parsley, thyme, and chives)
   ½ cup mayonnaise
   1 egg yolk
   1 teaspoon Dijon mustard
   1 teaspoon Worcestershire sauce
   ½ teaspoon Tabasco sauce
   Coarse salt, to taste
   Freshly ground black pepper, to taste
   ¼ cup (½ stick) unsalted butter

1. In a mixing bowl, combine artichokes, crabmeat, bread crumbs, onion, and herbs.

2. Add the mayonnaise, egg yolk, mustard, Worcestershire sauce, Tabasco, salt, and pepper. Mix thoroughly. Divide mixture into 8 large or 16 small crab cakes.

3. Heat butter in a hot sauté pan. Fry cakes till golden brown on each side. Serve immediately.

Note: Panko bread crumbs are coarser than those normally used in the United States and create a crunchier crust. They are sold in some supermarkets and most Asian markets.

Yield: 8 servings

Sonoma Goat Cheese Ravioli

A signature dish at the Contemporary resort's California Grill (page 86), it's been simplified here for you to re-create at home.

> 1 pound soft mild goat cheese (such as Montrachet), crumbled
> 5½ ounces aged goat cheese, crumbled
> ½ cup seasoned bread crumbs
> 2 tablespoons store-bought basil pesto
> 2 teaspoons extra-virgin olive oil
> 2 teaspoons Roasted Garlic Purée (recipe follows)
> ½ teaspoon salt, or to taste
> ⅛ teaspoon freshly ground black pepper, or to taste
> 16 egg roll wrappers
> 1 large egg and 1 tablespoon water, for egg wash
> Clear Tomato Broth (optional; recipe follows)

1. In a large bowl, stir together the fresh goat cheese, aged goat cheese, bread crumbs, pesto, olive oil, Roasted Garlic Purée, salt, and pepper until well combined.

2. On a work surface, lay out 8 egg roll wrappers and brush each with the egg wash. With a sharp knife, mark each wrapper into 4 squares, taking care not to cut all the way through. Place about 1 tablespoon of the goat cheese mixture in the center of each square. Cover with the 8 remaining egg roll wrappers and press the edges together. With a knife, cut each double wrapper with filling into 4 squares, to yield 32 squares of filled ravioli. Press the edges together. (If you are not using the ravioli immediately, sprinkle lightly with cornmeal, and store refrigerated between layers of waxed paper.)

3. When ready to serve, cook the ravioli in a large pot of salted boiling water for 1 to 2 minutes. Drain completely. Serve with Clear Tomato Broth, if you wish.

Yield: 4 to 6 servings

Roasted Garlic Purée

> 1 whole head of garlic
> 1 tablespoon olive oil

1. Preheat oven to 400°F.

2. Cut off the stem and top third of 1 whole garlic head. Remove peel.

3. Place garlic on a sheet of heavy-duty aluminum foil and drizzle with olive oil.

4. Wrap the garlic with foil, seal the edges tightly, and roast for 1 hour.

5. Remove the package from the oven, open carefully, and let the garlic cool slightly.

6. Scrape or squeeze out the pulp from the garlic cloves.

Clear Tomato Broth

> 15 whole, vine-ripened tomatoes
> 1 teaspoon salt

1. In a blender, in batches, coarsely chop the tomatoes with salt.

2. Place the chopped tomatoes in a large sieve lined with a double layer of damp cheesecloth, set it over a bowl, and let the mixture drain in the refrigerator for 24 hours to collect the liquid. Discard the tomato pulp and reserve the liquid.

Artist Point Berry Cobbler

Artist Point at Disney's Wilderness Lodge (page 109) takes diners on a culinary journey to the Pacific Northwest with regional recipes like this berry cobbler. (It's even better with a scoop of vanilla ice cream!)

1½ cups all-purpose flour
½ cup granulated sugar
2 teaspoons baking powder
½ teaspoon salt
½ cup (1 stick) plus 2 tablespoons cold
    butter, cut into small pieces
1 large egg
1 cup heavy cream
12 ounces fresh blueberries
2 tablespoons light brown sugar
½ pint *each* fresh raspberries and
    blackberries, and 8 strawberries

1. In a medium bowl, whisk together the flour, granulated sugar, baking powder, and salt. With a pastry blender, two knives used scissor style, or your hands, blend in ½ cup butter until crumbly. With a fork, stir in the egg and mix just enough to blend. Add heavy cream and mix just to incorporate; do not overmix.

2. Preheat oven to 350°F. Lightly grease a 9-inch cake pan, line the bottom with waxed paper, and grease the paper.

3. Press the dough evenly into the bottom of the cake pan. Place the blueberries on top of the dough and sprinkle with the brown sugar. Place the remaining butter pieces over the berries.

4. Bake for 20 to 25 minutes, or until golden brown. Cool on a wire rack. Remove the cake from the pan, cut in wedges, and serve with raspberries, blackberries, and strawberries.

Yield: 6 to 8 servings

Where to Find...

From french fries to filet mignon, fried chicken to chateaubriand, Disney dishes truly run the gamut. To help you zero in on the eateries that best fit your needs, we've created a handy index of specialized lists. Once you've settled on a particular spot, flip to its entry in the book to learn more about it. And if there's a category you'd like to see but don't— tell us and we'll try to include it in next year's book.

Bakeries/Pastry Shops

Beach Club Marketplace (Beach Club resort)
BoardWalk Bakery (BoardWalk resort)
Boulangerie Patisserie (Epcot, World Showcase)
Ice Cream and Bakery Shop (Epcot, The Land)
Kringla Bakeri og Kafe (Epcot, World Showcase)
Kusafiri Coffee Shop & Bakery (Animal Kingdom, Harambe)
Main Street Bakery (Magic Kingdom, Main Street, U.S.A.)
Starring Rolls Cafe (Disney's Hollywood Studios)

Barbecue

Flame Tree Barbecue (Animal Kingdom, DinoLand)
Mickey's Backyard Barbecue (see Dinner Shows, page 114)

Best Bang for the Buffet Buck (all-you-can-eat)

Biergarten (Epcot, World Showcase)
Boma—Flavors of Africa (Animal Kingdom Lodge)
Cape May Cafe (Beach Club resort)
Chef Mickey's (Contemporary resort)
Hollywood & Vine (Disney's Hollywood Studios)
1900 Park Fare (Grand Floridian resort)
Trail's End Restaurant (Fort Wilderness resort)
Tusker House (Animal Kingdom, Harambe)

Best with Babies (table-service)

Akershus Royal Banquet Hall (Epcot, World Showcase)
Biergarten (Epcot, World Showcase)
Chef Mickey's (Contemporary resort)
Crystal Palace (Magic Kingdom, Main Street, U.S.A.)
Donald's Safari Breakfast at Tusker House (Animal Kingdom, Harambe)
Garden Grill (Epcot, Future World)
Hollywood & Vine (Disney's Hollywood Studios)
'Ohana (Polynesian resort)
Olivia's Cafe (Disney's Old Key West resort)
Rainforest Cafe (Animal Kingdom and Downtown Disney)
Shutters at Old Port Royale (Caribbean Beach resort)
Tony's Town Square (Magic Kingdom, Main Street, U.S.A.)
Trail's End Restaurant (Fort Wilderness resort)

Brunch
House of Blues (Downtown Disney, West Side)

Buffet (all-you-can-eat)
Akershus Royal Banquet Hall (Epcot, World Showcase
  [appetizers only])
Biergarten (Epcot, World Showcase)
Boma—Flavors of Africa (Animal Kingdom Lodge)
Cape May Cafe (Beach Club resort)
Captain's Grille (breakfast only; Yacht Club resort)
Chef Mickey's (Contemporary resort)
Crystal Palace (Magic Kingdom, Main Street, U.S.A.)
Garden Grove (Swan resort)
Hollywood & Vine (Disney's Hollywood Studios)
1900 Park Fare (Grand Floridian resort)
Trail's End Restaurant (Fort Wilderness resort)
Tusker House (Animal Kingdom, Harambe)

Burgers
Backlot Express (Disney's Hollywood Studios)
Cabana Bar & Grill (Dolphin resort)
Capt. Cook's (Polynesian resort)
Cosmic Ray's Starlight Cafe (Magic Kingdom, Tomorrowland)
Electric Umbrella (Epcot, Future World)
ESPN Club (BoardWalk resort)
Everything Pop! (Pop Century resort)
Food Courts (All-Star resorts)
Fountain, The (Dolphin resort)
Gasparilla Grill & Games (Grand Floridian resort)
Liberty Inn (Epcot, World Showcase)
Old Port Royale (Caribbean Beach resort)
Pecos Bill Cafe (Magic Kingdom, Frontierland)
Planet Hollywood (Downtown Disney, West Side)
Restaurantosaurus (Animal Kingdom, DinoLand)
Riverside Mill (Port Orleans Riverside resort)
Roaring Fork (Wilderness Lodge)
Sassagoula Floatworks & Food Factory (Port Orleans
  French Quarter resort)
Sci-Fi Dine-In Theater (Disney's Hollywood Studios)
Sunset Ranch Market (Disney's Hollywood Studios)

Cheap Eats—Fast Food

Backlot Express (Disney's Hollywood Studios)
Casey's Corner (Magic Kingdom, Main Street, U.S.A.)
Columbia Harbour House (Magic Kingdom, Liberty Square)
Everything Pop! (Pop Century resort)
Flame Tree Barbecue (Animal Kingdom, DinoLand)
Restaurantosaurus (Animal Kingdom, Dinoland)
Sommerfest (Epcot, World Showcase)
Starring Rolls Cafe (Disney's Hollywood Studios)
Sunshine Seasons (Epcot, Future World)
Wolfgang Puck Express (Downtown Disney, Marketplace and West Side)
Yakitori House (Epcot, World Showcase)
Yorkshire County Fish Shop (Epcot, World Showcase)

Cheap Eats (relatively speaking)—Table-Service

Beaches & Cream Soda Shop (Beach Club resort)
Cap'n Jack's Restaurant (Downtown Disney, Marketplace)
Chef Mickey's (Contemporary resort)
ESPN Club (BoardWalk resort)
Olivia's Cafe (Disney's Old Key West resort)
Planet Hollywood (Downtown Disney, West Side)
Plaza Restaurant (Magic Kingdom, Main Street, U.S.A.)
Rainforest Cafe (Animal Kingdom and Downtown Disney, Marketplace)
Trail's End Restaurant (Fort Wilderness resort)
Tusker House (Animal Kingdom, Harambe)

Disney Characters (dining with)
(see page 103)

Ethnic Eateries
African

Boma—Flavors of Africa (Animal Kingdom Lodge)
Jiko—The Cooking Place (Animal Kingdom Lodge)
Marrakesh (Epcot, World Showcase)
Sanaa (Animal Kingdom Lodge, Kidani Village)
Tangierine Cafe (Epcot, World Showcase)
Tusker House (Animal Kingdom, Harambe)

American

Artist Point (Wilderness Lodge)
Big River Grille & Brewing Works (BoardWalk resort)
Boatwright's Dining Hall (Port Orleans Riverside resort)
California Grill (Contemporary resort)
ESPN Club (BoardWalk resort)
50's Prime Time Cafe (Disney's Hollywood Studios)
Flying Fish Cafe (BoardWalk resort)
Garden Grill (Epcot, Future World)
Grand Floridian Cafe (Grand Floridian resort)
Hollywood Brown Derby (Disney's Hollywood Studios)
House of Blues (Downtown Disney, West Side)
Liberty Inn (Epcot, World Showcase)
Liberty Tree Tavern (Magic Kingdom, Liberty Square)
Narcoossee's (Grand Floridian resort)
1900 Park Fare (Grand Floridian resort)
Olivia's Cafe (Old Key West resort)
Restaurantosaurus (Animal Kingdom, DinoLand)
Sci-Fi Dine-In Theater (Disney's Hollywood Studios)
Trail's End Restaurant (Fort Wilderness resort)
Wave, The (Contemporary resort)

British

Earl of Sandwich (Downtown Disney, Marketplace)
Rose & Crown Pub & Dining Room (Epcot, World Showcase)
Yorkshire County Fish Shop (Epcot, World Showcase)

Canadian

Le Cellier Steakhouse (Epcot, World Showcase)

Chinese and Southeast Asian

Lotus Blossom Cafe (Epcot, World Showcase)
Nine Dragons (Epcot, World Showcase)
Yak & Yeti (Animal Kingdom, Asia)

Cuban

Bongos Cuban Cafe (Downtown Disney, West Side)

French

Bistro de Paris (Epcot, World Showcase)
Boulangerie Patisserie (Epcot, World Showcase)
Chefs de France (Epcot, World Showcase)

German

Biergarten (Epcot, World Showcase)
Sommerfest (Epcot, World Showcase)

Italian/Mediterranean

Il Mulino New York Trattoria (Swan resort)
Kouzzina by Cat Cora (BoardWalk resort)
Mama Melrose's Ristorante Italiano (Disney's Hollywood
   Studios)
Pizzafari (Animal Kingdom, Discovery Island)
Portobello (Downtown Disney, Pleasure Island)
Tony's Town Square (Magic Kingdom, Main Street, U.S.A.)

Japanese

Kimonos (Swan resort)
Mitsukoshi's Teppan Edo (Epcot, World Showcase)
Mitsukoshi's Tokyo Dining (Epcot, World Showcase)
Yakitori House (Epcot, World Showcase)

Mexican/Latin American

Cantina de San Angel (Epcot, World Showcase)
El Pirata y el Perico (Magic Kingdom, Adventureland)
Maya Grill (Coronado Springs resort)
San Angel Inn (Epcot, World Showcase)

Norwegian

Akershus Royal Banquet Hall (Epcot, World Showcase)
Kringla Bakeri og Kafe (Epcot, World Showcase)

WHERE TO FIND

Family-style (all-you-can-eat)

Akershus Royal Banquet Hall (Epcot, World Showcase)
Garden Grill (Epcot, Future World)
Garden Grove (Swan resort)
Hoop-Dee-Doo Musical Revue (see page 114)
Liberty Tree Tavern (Magic Kingdom, Liberty Square)
Mickey's Backyard Barbecue (see page 114)
'Ohana (Polynesian resort)
Spirit of Aloha (see page 115)
Tusker House (Animal Kingdom, Harambe)
Whispering Canyon Cafe (Wilderness Lodge)

Fruit

Aloha Isle (Magic Kingdom, Adventureland)
Harambe Fruit Market (Animal Kingdom, Harambe)
Liberty Square Market (Magic Kingdom, Liberty Square)
Sunset Ranch Market (Disney's Hollywood Studios)
Toontown Farmers Market (Magic Kingdom, Mickey's
  Toontown Fair)

Good for Groups

Biergarten (Epcot, World Showcase)
Boma—Flavors of Africa (Animal Kingdom Lodge)
California Grill (Contemporary resort)
Crystal Palace (Magic Kingdom, Main Street, U.S.A.)
Flame Tree Barbecue (Animal Kingdom, DinoLand)
Hollywood & Vine (Disney's Hollywood Studios)
House of Blues (Downtown Disney, West Side)
Mickey's Backyard Barbecue (see page 114)
Mitsukoshi's Teppan Edo (Epcot, World Showcase)
'Ohana (Polynesian resort)
Raglan Road (Downtown Disney, Pleasure Island)
Sunshine Seasons (Epcot, Future World)
Tusker House (Animal Kingdom, Harambe)
Wave, The (Contemporary resort)
Wolfgang Puck Café (Downtown Disney, West Side)
Wolfgang Puck Café—The Dining Room (Downtown
  Disney, West Side)
Yachtsman Steakhouse (Yacht Club resort)

Hot Dogs

Backlot Express (Disney's Hollywood Studios)
Casey's Corner (Magic Kingdom, Main Street, U.S.A.)
Liberty Inn (Epcot, World Showcase)
Mara, The (Animal Kingdom Lodge)
Studio Catering Co. (Disney's Hollywood Studios)
Sunset Ranch Market (Disney's Hollywood Studios)
Wetzel's Pretzels (Downtown Disney, Marketplace and
  West Side)

Ice Cream and Frozen Treats

Aloha Isle (Magic Kingdom, Adventureland)

Anandapur Ice Cream Truck (Animal Kingdom, Asia)
Beaches & Cream Soda Shop (Beach Club resort)
Cool Post (Epcot, World Showcase)
Enchanted Grove (Magic Kingdom, Fantasyland)
Ghirardelli Ice Cream & Chocolate Shop (Downtown Disney, Marketplace)
Hollywood Scoops (Disney's Hollywood Studios)
Min & Bill's Dockside Diner (Disney's Hollywood Studios)
Mrs. Potts' Cupboard (Magic Kingdom, Fantasyland)
Plaza Ice Cream Parlor (Magic Kingdom, Main Street, U.S.A.)
Plaza Restaurant (Magic Kingdom, Main Street, U.S.A.)
Scuttle's Landing (Magic Kingdom, Fantasyland)
Seashore Sweets (BoardWalk resort)
Sunshine Tree Terrace (Magic Kingdom, Adventureland)

Kids' Favorites

Akershus Royal Banquet Hall (Epcot, World Showcase)
Casey's Corner (Magic Kingdom, Main Street, U.S.A.)
Chef Mickey's (Contemporary resort)
Cinderella's Royal Table (Magic Kingdom, Fantasyland)
Crystal Palace (Magic Kingdom, Main Street, U.S.A.)
50's Prime Time Cafe (Disney's Hollywood Studios)
Garden Grill (Epcot, Future World)
Hoop-Dee-Doo Musical Revue (see page 114)
Liberty Inn (Epcot, World Showcase)
1900 Park Fare (Grand Floridian resort)
'Ohana (Polynesian resort)
Pecos Bill Cafe (Magic Kingdom, Frontierland)
Pinocchio Village Haus (Magic Kingdom, Fantasyland)
Pizza Planet (Disney's Hollywood Studios)
Pizzafari (Animal Kingdom, Discovery Island)
Planet Hollywood (Downtown Disney, West Side)
Rainforest Cafe (Animal Kingdom and Downtown Disney, Marketplace)
Sci-Fi Dine-In Theater (Disney's Hollywood Studios)
Sunset Ranch Market (Disney's Hollywood Studios)
Sunshine Seasons (Epcot, Future World)
T-Rex: A Prehistoric Family Adventure (Downtown Disney, Marketplace)
Tusker House (Animal Kingdom, Harambe)
Whispering Canyon Cafe (Wilderness Lodge)

Knockout Views

Big River Grille & Brewing Works (outdoor seating; BoardWalk resort)
California Grill (Contemporary resort)
Cantina de San Angel (Epcot, World Showcase)
Casey's Corner (Magic Kingdom, Main Street, U.S.A.)
Coral Reef (Epcot, Future World)
Narcoossee's (Grand Floridian resort)
Rose & Crown Pub & Dining Room (Epcot, World Showcase)

Kosher (fast-food selections)

ABC Commissary (Disney's Hollywood Studios)
Artist's Palette (Saratoga Springs resort)
Cosmic Ray's Starlight Cafe (Magic Kingdom, Tomorrowland)
Everything Pop! (Pop Century resort)
Food Courts (All-Star and Port Orleans Riverside resorts)
Gasparilla's (Grand Floridian resort)
Liberty Inn (Epcot, World Showcase)
Mara, The (Animal Kingdom Lodge)
Old Port Royale (Caribbean Beach resort)
Pizzafari (Animal Kingdom, Discovery Island)
Roaring Fork (Wilderness Lodge)

Lounges and Bars (with food)

Barefoot Bar (Polynesian resort)
Big River Grille & Brewing Works (BoardWalk resort)
Bongos Cuban Cafe (Downtown Disney, West Side)
Cabana Bar & Grill (Dolphin resort)
California Grill Lounge (Contemporary resort)
Capetown Lounge and Wine Bar (inside Jiko—The Cooking Place; Animal Kingdom Lodge)
Cap'n Jack's Restaurant (Downtown Disney, Marketplace)
Crew's Cup (Yacht Club resort)
Crockett's Tavern (Fort Wilderness resort)
ESPN Club (BoardWalk resort)
Garden View (Grand Floridian resort)
Hurricane Hanna's Grille (Yacht & Beach Club resorts)
Il Mulino New York Trattoria Lounge (Swan resort)
Kimonos (Swan resort)
Leaping Horse Libations (BoardWalk resort)
Mardi Grogs (Port Orleans French Quarter resort)

Martha's Vineyard (Beach Club resort)
Mizner's (Grand Floridian resort)
Muddy Rivers (Port Orleans Riverside resort)
Narcoossee's (Grand Floridian resort)
Outer Rim (Contemporary resort)
Portobello (Downtown Disney, Pleasure Island)
Rainforest Cafe (Magic Mushroom bar; Animal Kingdom and Downtown Disney, Marketplace)
Raglan Road (Downtown Disney, Pleasure Island)
River Roost (Port Orleans Riverside resort)
Rix Lounge (Coronado Springs resort)
Rose & Crown Pub (Epcot, World Showcase)
Sand Bar (Contemporary resort)
Siestas (Coronado Springs resort)
Sommerfest (Inside Germany; Epcot, World Showcase)
Splash Terrace (Swan resort)
Stone Crab Lounge (Inside Fulton's Crab House; Downtown Disney, Pleasure Island)
Tambu Lounge (Polynesian resort)
Territory Lounge (Wilderness Lodge)
Tune-In Lounge (Disney's Hollywood Studios)
Turtle Shack (Disney's Old Key West resort)
Uzima Springs (Animal Kingdom Lodge)

New to WDW

Sanaa (Animal Kingdom Lodge)
Kouzzina by Cat Cora (BoardWalk resort)

Open 24 Hours

Capt. Cook's (Polynesian resort)
Gasparilla Grill & Games (Grand Floridian resort)

DID YOU KNOW?

The Contemporary resort's California Grill serves about 70 pounds of tomatoes *every night* during tomato season (July through November).

Picabu (Dolphin resort)
Sundial Cafe 24-7 (Regal Sun hotel)

Pizza

Capt. Cook's (Polynesian resort)
Everything Pop! (Pop Century resort)
Food Courts (All-Star resorts)
Gasparilla Grill & Games (Grand Floridian resort)
Mama Melrose's Ristorante Italiano (Disney's Hollywood
   Studios)
Pinocchio Village Haus (Magic Kingdom, Fantasyland)
Pizzafari (Animal Kingdom, Discovery Island)
Pizza Planet (Disney's Hollywood Studios)
Planet Hollywood (Downtown Disney, West Side)
Riverside Mill (Port Orleans Riverside resort)
Roaring Fork (Wilderness Lodge)
Royale Pizza Shop (Caribbean Beach resort)
Sassagoula Floatworks & Food Factory (Port Orleans
   French Quarter resort)
Sunset Ranch Market (Disney's Hollywood Studios)
Trail's End Restaurant (Fort Wilderness resort)
Wolfgang Puck Café (Downtown Disney, West Side)
Wolfgang Puck Express (Downtown Disney, Marketplace
   and West Side)

Salads

Artist's Palette (Saratoga Springs resort)
Big River Grille & Brewing Works (BoardWalk resort)
Boma—Flavors of Africa (Animal Kingdom Lodge)
Cape May Cafe (Beach Club resort)
Chef Mickey's (Contemporary resort)
Cinderella's Royal Table (Magic Kingdom, Fantasyland)
Columbia Harbour House (Magic Kingdom, Liberty Square)
Cosmic Ray's Starlight Cafe (Magic Kingdom,
   Tomorrowland)
Crystal Palace (Magic Kingdom, Main Street, U.S.A.)
Flame Tree Barbecue (Animal Kingdom, DinoLand)
Hollywood Brown Derby (Disney's Hollywood Studios)
Il Mulino New York Trattoria (Swan resort)
Le Cellier Steakhouse (Epcot, World Showcase)
1900 Park Fare (Grand Floridian resort)

Pecos Bill Cafe (Magic Kingdom, Frontierland)
Pepper Market (Coronado Springs resort)
Pinocchio Village Haus (Magic Kingdom, Fantasyland)
Plaza Restaurant (Magic Kingdom, Main Street, U.S.A.)
Rainforest Cafe (Animal Kingdom and Downtown Disney,
   Marketplace)
Sunshine Seasons (Epcot, Future World)
Wave, The (Contemporary resort)
Wolfgang Puck Café (Downtown Disney, West Side)

Seafood

Artist Point (Wilderness Lodge)
Cape May Cafe (Beach Club resort)
Cap'n Jack's Restaurant (Downtown Disney, Marketplace)
Columbia Harbour House (Magic Kingdom, Liberty Square)
Coral Reef (Epcot, Future World)
Flying Fish Cafe (BoardWalk resort)
Fulton's Crab House (Downtown Disney, Pleasure Island)
Narcoossee's (Grand Floridian resort)
Todd English's bluezoo (Dolphin resort)
Wave, The (Contemporary resort)

Snack Bars (at the resorts)

Beach Club Marketplace (Beach Club resort)
Cabana Bar & Grill (Dolphin resort)
Capt. Cook's (Polynesian resort)
Contempo (Contemporary resort)
Gasparilla Grill & Games (Grand Floridian resort)
Hurricane Hanna's Grill (Yacht Club resort)
Mara, The (Animal Kingdom Lodge)
Picabu (Dolphin resort)
Roaring Fork (Wilderness Lodge)
Sand Bar (pool bar; Contemporary resort)

Solo Diners

Cap'n Jack's Restaurant (Downtown Disney, Marketplace)
Crew's Cup (lounge, Yacht Club resort)
ESPN Club (BoardWalk resort)
Flying Fish Cafe (BoardWalk resort)
Il Mulino New York Trattoria (Swan resort)
Stone Crab Lounge (inside Fulton's Crab House, Downtown

Disney, Pleasure Island)
Tune-In Lounge (Disney's Hollywood Studios)
Wolfgang Puck Café Bar (Downtown Disney, West Side)

Steak
Captain's Grille (Yacht Club resort)
Le Cellier Steakhouse (Epcot, World Showcase)
Shula's Steak House (Dolphin resort)
Yachtsman Steakhouse (Yacht Club resort)

Super Splurges (for grown-ups)
Artist Point (Wilderness Lodge)
Bistro de Paris (Epcot, World Showcase)
California Grill (Contemporary resort)
Chefs de France (Epcot, World Showcase)
Jiko—The Cooking Place (Animal Kingdom Lodge)
Shula's Steak House (Dolphin resort)
Victoria & Albert's (Grand Floridian resort)
Wolfgang Puck Café—The Dining Room (Downtown
  Disney, West Side)
Yachtsman Steakhouse (Yacht Club resort)

Sushi
California Grill (Contemporary resort)
Capt. Cook's (Polynesian resort)
Kimonos (lounge; Swan resort)
Mitsukoshi's Tokyo Dining (Epcot, World Showcase)
Wolfgang Puck Café (Downtown Disney, West Side)
Yakitori House (Epcot, World Showcase)

Terrific Theming
Akershus Royal Banquet Hall (Epcot, World Showcase)
Biergarten (Epcot, World Showcase)
Cinderella's Royal Table (Magic Kingdom, Fantasyland)
50's Prime Time Cafe (Disney's Hollywood Studios)
Liberty Tree Tavern (Magic Kingdom, Liberty Square)
'Ohana (Polynesian resort)
Rainforest Cafe (Animal Kingdom and Downtown Disney,
  Marketplace)
Sci-Fi Dine-In Theater (Disney's Hollywood Studios)

T-Rex: A Prehistoric Family Adventure (Downtown Disney, Marketplace)

Vegetarian Selections
Boma—Flavors of Africa (Animal Kingdom Lodge)
Columbia Harbour House (Magic Kingdom, Liberty Square)
Cosmic Ray's Starlight Cafe (Magic Kingdom, Tomorrowland)
Everything Pop! (Pop Century resort)
Food Courts (All-Star resorts)
Mama Melrose's Ristorante Italiano (Disney's Hollywood Studios)
Marrakesh (Epcot, World Showcase)
Pizzafari (Animal Kingdom, Discovery Island)
Planet Hollywood (Downtown Disney, West Side)
Rainforest Cafe (Animal Kingdom and Downtown Disney, Marketplace)
Sunset Ranch Market (Disney's Hollywood Studios)
Sunshine Seasons (Epcot, Future World)
Tony's Town Square (Magic Kingdom, Main Street, U.S.A.)
Tusker House (Animal Kingdom, Harambe)
Wolfgang Puck Express (Downtown Disney, West Side and Marketplace)

Wine and Dine (great wine lists)
Artist Point (Wilderness Lodge)
Boma—Flavors of Africa (Animal Kingdom Lodge)
California Grill (Contemporary resort)
Chefs de France (Epcot, World Showcase)
Citricos (Grand Floridian resort)
Flying Fish Cafe (BoardWalk resort)
Hollywood Brown Derby (Disney's Hollywood Studios)
Il Mulino New York Trattoria (Swan resort)
Jiko—The Cooking Place (Animal Kingdom Lodge)
Narcoossee's (Grand Floridian resort)
Portobello (Downtown Disney, Pleasure Island)
Shula's Steak House (Dolphin resort)
Victoria & Albert's (Grand Floridian resort)
Wave, The (Contemporary resort)
Wolfgang Puck Café—The Dining Room (Downtown Disney, West Side)
Yachtsman Steakhouse (Yacht Club resort)

Index

INDEX

INDEX